Stock Market:

How to Invest and Trade in the Stok Market Like a Pro

Andrew Johnson
© 2017

Sign Up & Join
<u>Andrew Johnson's</u>
<u>Mailing List!</u>

*EXCLUSIVE UPDATES

*FREE BOOKS

*NEW REALEASE ANNOUCEMENTS BEFORE ANYONE ELSE GETS THEM

*DISCOUNTS

*GIVEAWAYS

FOR NOTIFACTIONS OF MY <u>*NEW RELEASES*</u> :

Never miss my next FREE PROMO, my next NEW RELEASE or a GIVEAWAY!

in any fashion deemed liable for any hardship or damages that may befall them after undertaking information described herein.

Additionally, the information found on the following pages is intended for informational purposes only and should thus be considered, universal. As befitting its nature, the information presented is without assurance regarding its continued validity or interim quality. Trademarks that mentioned are done without written consent and can in no way be considered an endorsement from the trademark holder.

THIS BUNDLE INCLUDES THE FOLLOWING BOOKS:

Day Trading: The Ultimate Guide to Day Trading: Uncovering Day Trading Profit Making Secrets

AND

Options Trading: The Ultimate Guide to Options Trading: Uncovering Options Trading Profit Making Secrets

AND

A Beginner's Guide to Day Trading: Discover How to Be a Day Trading King

AND

Options Trading: A Beginners Guide to Option Trading Unlocking the Secrets of Option Trading

AND

Day Trading: Strategies on How to Excel at Day Trading

AND

Options Trading: Strategies on How to Excel at Options Trading

TABLE OF CONTENTS

DAY TRADING: THE ULTIMATE GUIDE TO DAY TRADING: UNCOVERING DAY TRADING PROFIT MAKING SECRETS

DESCRIPTION

While anyone can make a few trades per day, and maybe even find some success while doing so, if you are interested in day trading on a serious level then there are many distinctive characteristics and traits that you should strive to embody on a regular basis. Likewise, there are certain strategies you should know in order to give yourself a fighting chance. If you are interested in doing more than simply surviving in the world of day trading, if you are looking to truly thrive then *Day Trading: The Ultimate Guide to Day Trading* is the book that you have been waiting for.

Inside you will find everything you need to up your day trading game as quickly and effectively as possible. This includes characteristics that all good day traders should possess and how to implement them in your own life. You will also find important tips and tricks to maximize your overall trade effectiveness as well as frequently made mistakes and the easiest ways to ensure that you don't fall into their traps.

You will also find a complete breakdown of the tools that every competent day trader needs as well as specific suggestions to ensure that know what the professionals are using and where to find them. Finally, you will find five of the most effective strategies for gaining success while day trading with in-depth explanations to ensure you can put them into action ASAP. It doesn't matter what markets, timeframes or risk/reward ratios that you favor, *Day Trading: The Ultimate Guide to Day Trading* has the right strategy for you.

Being a successful day trader is all about having the knowledge, not just to know where the market is going but how to best take advantage of where it's been. This is what separates the novices from the experts and those that boast a successful trade percentage from those who wouldn't be able to trade at a 50 percent success rate if their lives depended on it. So, what are you waiting for? Get ready to tap into that knowledge and buy this book today.

Inside you will find

- The importance of finding a way to motivate yourself without worrying about external stimuli
- Tips for successfully choosing the right trade at the right time a statistically relevant portion of the time
- The importance of timing and how to ensure you always choose the right time to enter or exit a trade
- The five most important attributes for every successful day trader to have and how to implement them in your own life
- The difference between the butterfly spread and the modified butterfly spread and when to use each for the best results

- What value areas are and how to put them to work effectively for you
- Why you shouldn't be trading options without considering hedging your trades
- How scalping Bollinger bands can take your forex trading game to the next level while only increasing your risk a small amount
- The best way to jump into futures trading while maintaining a reasonable level of risk
- *And more...*

INTRODUCTION

Congratulations on downloading *Day Trading: The Ultimate Guide to Day Trading* and thank you for doing so. For many traders, even those who are experienced working in various markets, taking the next step and day trading can be a daunting process. The speed at which day trading takes place, coupled with the much greater potential for loss, as well as gains, means that you would do well to learn as much as possible before diving in.

To that end, the following chapters will discuss everything you know to begin day trading on the right foot. First, you will learn about many of the characteristics that successful day traders embody. Next, you will learn tips for ensuring that your time spent day trading is as effective as possible as well as common mistakes that many day traders make so that you don't fall into these common traps yourself. You will then learn about many of the tools that are crucial to a day trader's success including specific options to consider based on what is currently popular with the day trading crowd.

With the generalities out of the way, you will then read in-depth accounts concerning five different day trading strategies including the modified butterfly spread, value areas and order flow sequencing, forex options hedging, scalping Bollinger bands and trading future spreads. Each of these strategies will go beyond the basics in an effort to provide you with all the details to put them into practice yourself in an effort to maximize your profits as effortlessly as possible.

There are plenty of books on this subject on the market, thanks again for choosing this one! Every effort was made to ensure it is full of as much useful information as possible, please enjoy!

CHAPTER 1: SUCCESSFUL DAY TRADER CHARACTERISTICS

While making a few successful trades every day is relatively straightforward, if you hope to take your skills to the next level there are several things you can strive to do to maximize your success. No two day traders are exactly alike, but the most successful in the field tend to exhibit many of the same positive traits and characteristics outlined below.

Get a jump on the day: Just because the market doesn't open until 9:30 am, that doesn't mean this is when your day should begin. Successful traders spend the early morning hours checking in on the international markets so they know what the day is likely to bring. The Western economy doesn't exist in a vacuum, understanding the foreign markets makes it easier to predict upcoming changes at home. Remember, having an accurate macro view is a key part of utilizing micro changes effectively.

Become a master: In order to truly master a new skill, be it ballroom dancing or day trading, you need to be willing to put in the practice time. It takes 10,000 hours to become a true master which works out to eight hours a day for 42 months. While certain people are always going to get lucky, if you hope to see significant success you have to be willing to put in the work up front. Day trading is a marathon, not a sprint, slow and steady wins the race.

Never stop learning: The most successful day traders are not the ones who have mastered existing plans and strategies, they are the ones who understand that new alternatives are always taking shape. Getting in the habit of always remaining on the lookout for the next big thing is one of the best ways to separate yourself from the amateur day traders who will never be truly successful. The market is constantly in flux which means that any analysis you do is going to have a shelf life of less a week, at most. Resting on your laurels when it comes to what you know is a surefire way to curtail your profits. Remember, learning leads to earning.

Forge your own path: The best day traders don't just automatically go along with the crowd. They trust their intuition and their research, even if it means making trades that aren't on anyone else's radar. The biggest wins come from trades that are against the mainstream and knowing when to execute is what separates average traders from masters. The key here is to know the difference between trades that have been hyped up and those that have potential based on facts alone. Much daily market movement is caused by sheep who follow what the crowd is doing, be a wolf instead. If you don't feel as though your intuition is as strong as it could be, the solution is to keep studying and do more trading. Early success will improve your confidence and make it easier to trust in yourself no matter what.

Be ready for anything: The best traders are the ones that know they have a quality plan and also have the ability to stick to it without letting their emotions get in the way. There is more to being successful than blindly following your plan, however, you also need to be capable of understanding when things have changed enough to make it irrelevant. The easiest way to do this is to know the state of the market as it currently stands and where it is likely to go while the trading day is in progress. Whatever you do, it is important to keep a firm grip on your emotions as there is no quicker way to fail than to start thinking with your heart as opposed to your head.

Know yourself: In order to be a successful trader in the long term, it is crucial that you understand your strengths as well as your weaknesses. Doing so will enable you to capitalize on the one while shoring up the other. This is a key part of minimizing risk; which, in turn, is key to maximizing your profits. The easiest way to go about determining what your strengths and weaknesses are is to keep a trading journal. Keeping tabs on all the specifics related to each trade you make will allow you to look for patterns that otherwise might remain hidden. Once you are aware of any negative patterns you might fall into, you will be well on your way to mitigating them.

Know when to act: You can do all the research you like, if you don't have the ability to pull the trigger when the time is right then you will never be a successful day trader. The market is fickle, especially in the charts that day traders favor, which means that huge gains or losses can occur in moments. As such, you need to be able to make split second decisions and know that they are the right ones when money is on the line. This isn't the same as following your gut or getting lucky, it is the skill to read new situations and react in real time and to be able to do so effectively time and again.

Internal motivation: In order to be a successful day trader, you need to be able to motivate yourself to keep at it, even when the going gets tough. Making trading your job means that there will be no one looking over your shoulder telling you to get to work, that motivation will need to come from within. Only by looking within and finding the personal drive to succeed will you be able to do what needs to be done regardless of the cost. This is where the discipline to go from good to great comes from and it is not something that can be learned, you are either self-motivated or you aren't.

Have enough trading capital: In order to be a successful day trader you need to have the right amount of capital at your disposal. If every trade is life or death then this will skew your motivation and potentially keep you from making trades that will likely be successful. The most successful traders know their limits and never step outside them. No trader can be right one hundred percent of the time, and when the odds aren't in your favor you need to know that you can come back from the loss and try again. This is why it is recommended that you never put more than two percent of your total trading capital into a single trade. Sticking to this rule will keep your potential for loss at a reasonable level and help to ensure that you are able to manage your emotions at all times. Ensuring an emotional distance from all of your trades means that you will always be able to listen to reason, improving your overall trade percentage in the process.

Never be afraid to think things through: While making split-second trades is crucial to finding success as a day trader, that doesn't mean you should do so without thinking the state of things through first. It is important to always know exactly what your decisions are going to lead to, even if it means missing out of the maximum amount of potential profit to do so. While trading, your goal should always be to make decisions that are proactive, never reactive.

CHAPTER 2: TIPS TO MAKE DAY TRADING AS PROFITABLE AS POSSIBLE

While day trading successfully is always going to involve a little luck, that doesn't mean there is nothing you can do to improve your averages. Consider the following tips and tricks to help you end every day further in the black than when you started.

Choosing the right trades

A successful trade is always going to be built on a measured approach. To ensure this is the case you are going to want to begin by choosing the type of stocks that align with your goals as well as your temperament. Furthermore, you are going to want to take any external knowledge you might have into account when choosing the right stocks to focus on. As an example, if you were previously in the medical field then stocks based on pharmaceutical companies might be a good choice. Regardless, it is important to always take the following three main aspects of every trade into account before you make any decisions.

Timeframe: First and foremost, you are always going to want to trade in a timeframe that you are comfortable with. Doing otherwise will simply lead to scenarios where you are not at your best because you are impatient or just plain nervous. If you are still trying to improve your overall trade percentage you will likely want to stick to the 5-minute charts until you can be truly comfortable dealing with the potential for risk that holding stocks overnight can cause. You will also need to consider if you prefer micromanaging trades all day every day or prefer doing all your research over the weekend to pursue weekly trades come Monday morning. Micromanaging trades leads to short-term gains while weekly trades produce long-term gains.

Trading tactics: When it comes to choosing a methodology to use while trading, it is important to focus on what works for you instead of bouncing around based on what is popular in the moment. It is important to remember that every trader is going to have good days and bad days and if you can find a methodology that is successful at least 60 percent of the time then you are well on your way to success. Switching your tactics constantly is only going to skew your stats so you won't be able to determine the true cause of either your successes or your failures. What's worse, changing constantly will make it difficult for you to learn the intricacies of the methodologies you use, meaning they will be less effective in even more scenarios.

Tools of the trade: Much like methodologies, it is important to find a few trading instruments that work for you and focus on making the most of them. This is preferable to using a little bit of everything as you will be able to more closely tailor what you use to match your trading style. The best way to determine what is going to be useful to your style is by focusing on instruments that match the timeframes you frequent most often.

Attributes

There are several different attributes that all day traders should strive to embody. While not everyone will naturally be able to access them from the start, they can all be improved with practice.

Patience: After you have found a trade that you think is going to be fruitful, it is important to exhibit patience and find the perfect moment to pull the trigger. This is why it is useful to always determine your entry and exit points beforehand, so that there is less of a chance of emotion getting in the way. Additionally, if the trade doesn't reach those numbers then you need to have the patience to wait for a better option to come along. If you decide to chase the potential for profit by altering your exit and entry points on the fly then all you are going to do is to skew the effectiveness of your plan. Once this occurs you lose regardless of the outcome as even if you profit from the sudden change you are reinforcing bad habits that will ultimately cause you harm in the long run.

Belief: Having belief in the trading plan or system that you have created is crucial when it comes to day trading because no plan is flawless. Day trading plans only prove successful when used reliably in the long term and swapping things around constantly is going to skew the percentages against you. Remember, a good plan or system gives you an edge, otherwise you are essentially just gambling and there are more effective ways to gamble than with the stock market. Believe in yourself and your system and you will see greater profits overall.

Objectivity: It is important to never get too attached to a given stock and always approach every trade from a point of objectivity. Losing this objectivity can cause you to make mistakes like doubling down on a stock that has gone out of the money or staying in past the logical exit point. The same goes for listening to outside sources. Once you have committed to a given trade the only source you will want to listen to is your trading plan, everything else may as well be white noise. Each trade should be analyzed based on its relative merits, if you do so then you should trust yourself and let the rest take care of itself.

Expectations: Believing in yourself is an important part of day trading successfully but having measured expectations is crucial as well. Above all you need to have a realistic understanding of what your profits are likely to be before you start any new trade. Having realistic expectations in this way will help to prevent you from letting emotions get the better of you and lead to more reliable trades overall. Keeping your expectations in check means understanding the risk and reward of every trade. Remember, short term trades are more likely to lead to small, safe gains while long term trades are riskier and can end in greater gains.

Motivations: It is important to understand your own motivations in order to be true to yourself and your trading style. It is also important to understand the various motivations that different commodity markets have if you hope to trade in them successfully. In order to determine the current motivations of the commodities you favor, the first thing you will want to do is to consider the major players in the market in question. With that in mind, you can then watch the commodities themselves and determine how they are moving and why. Once you are familiar with what is currently happening you can then compare that to the historical movement. When taken as a whole you can then determine how the moves the major players make affect changing market conditions and predict future movement from there.

Putting thoughts into action

Keeping everything in mind at all times can be challenging, if you never put what you have learned into practice, however, then you will never grow as a trader. What's worse, you will never turn a reliable profit. Once you know what you are doing you will then want to keep track of your trades as soon as they begin and don't be afraid to bail on a trade when it suddenly goes south. Remember, a small loss now is always preferable to a bigger loss in the future. Additionally, it is important to keep in mind that there will not always be a worthwhile trade to be made. Just because you are a day trader doesn't mean you need to be trading every second of every day.

Learning the most intricate parts of the markets you favor isn't something that can be taught, it can only be learned with practice. What's more, sometimes mood is going to skew unexpectedly and through everything out the window for a time. Ultimately it all comes down to Warren Buffet's number one rule, "the only hard and fast rule is to never lose money." Stick to this rule and you can never go wrong.

CHAPTER 3: IMPORTANT DAY TRADING MISTAKES TO AVOID

While it is impossible to become a master day trader without making, and learning from, mistakes. There are plenty of pitfalls that being aware of will allow you to avoid without stepping into them yourself. Remember, forewarned is forearmed.

Chasing tops and bottoms: Some strategies are effective when put into play near potential turning points. These are in the minority however and picking tops or bottoms is a risky proposition, at best. It is common for many traders to invest extra money into securities that seem either too low or too high, breaking the cardinal rule of a two percent trading limit in the process. This impulse should be avoided at all cost in favor of focusing on the major move that is inbound. Starting to one side of range-bound markets will lead to better overall results practically all of the time.

Not getting while the getting is good: Many day traders have an adequate entry plan but then move forward without determining an exit plan that is just as effective. This, in turn, leads to scenarios where they either get out too early, too late or end up with an investment instead of a trade. If you find it difficult to know when to exit gracefully, you will want to focus on adding detailed technical specifications to your exit strategy. Once you put these specifics into place, it is important to monitor them and change them as needed as the market evolves.

Wasting time trying to get even: If you ever hope to be a master day trader then you need to factor failure into your long-term plan. Not only will this make it easier to prevent emotion from getting the better of you, it will help you make fewer mistakes down the line as well. Remember, it is important to focus exclusively on the numbers and not pin your self-esteem or personal image to individual trades. Focusing on the price action will allow you to block out thoughts about breaking even or magic numbers and improve your trade percentage as a result. Determining if a day was a success or a failure isn't something you can do until the market closes and it is useless, and destructive, to try.

Following relative trends: Existing trends in the market can be a potential signpost for future movement but they are far from guaranteed. It is completely natural for the market to fluctuate as much as 20 percent on either side of the average at any given time. As such, if you jump on an apparent trend without researching it thoroughly you can find yourself attached to a momentum play that will never materialize. Instead, it is important to consider each apparent trend through the lens of three distinct time frames for the best results. If you are fond of short-term trades then daily, hourly and weekly charts are recommended. If you prefer long-term trades then you will want to stick to weekly, daily, and monthly charts instead.

Unduly narrowing your focus: Every time you make a trade it is important to remember that it doesn't exist in a vacuum. Not taking this into account will cut into your trading capital with a steady stream of preventable losses. A better solution is to instead take a macro view on all of your current trades. This means keeping tabs on market leads and looking for capital that is likely to move in general derivatives. These derivatives are key as they highlight the underlying connections between markets that ensure they move in the same ways. Remember, the greater your scope the more effective you will be.

Letting strong opinions affect your trading: While everyone has opinions, effective day traders know that letting them influence your daily trades is a recipe for disaster. The only thing you need to rely on in order to trade effectively is math, anything else is just going to get in the way. Observe and analyze political and economic events, don't get caught up in them.

 *Having the wrong timing:* Finding a potentially profitable trade is only half the battle, you also need to learn when to pull the trigger for the best results. Making the right move at the wrong time costs day traders collectively millions of dollars a day. This is not to say that you need to wait for everything to align perfectly before you make your move. Rather, you are going to want to get a feel for the moment that things are right enough and act accordingly.

To do so you are going to want to be aware of relative trend, understand the current strength of the weekly cycle and keep an eye on accumulation and distribution indicators. Above all else, never move on a hunch or tip without doing the required research as all you are likely to do is throw your commission fees away.

Averaging down: While averaging down is rarely the primary plan, it is easy to let it happen if you aren't actively planning against it. The resources spent holding a weak position can almost always be better spent elsewhere as every trade costs you time and weak positions are likely to cost you money as well. Keep in mind that every failed trade means that your next successful trade needs to pay out extra just to help you break even for the day and then even more to get ahead. If your starting trade capital isn't that great, averaging down can represent days, or even weeks, you are going to need to spend crawling back to square one. If you subsist on short-term trades then you need to be ready to exit as soon as forward momentum slows or, at worst, starts to slip backward.

Not accurately calculating risk and reward: Risk and reward are naturally a part of every trade. This doesn't mean they are always equal, however, and if you don't take the difference into account you can make the wrong moves without even realizing it. This is why it is important to set daily trading limits as it will help you to bring things into focus. If a given trade is risky enough to warrant possibly losing ten percent of your daily loss limit then you will want to ensure it will pay out at least twice, if not three times as much to balance out the risk. Regardless, making ten smaller trades that are more likely to be successful is almost always going to be a better choice.

CHAPTER 4: THE BEST TOOLS OF THE TRADE

 Perhaps more so than any other type of trading, the tools you employ while day trading are extremely important if you hope to turn a profit on a regular basis. Due to the tight timeframes that day traders operate under, every second counts which is why the tools, software and platforms outlined below bear serious consideration.

Tools

Current hardware: You don't necessarily need a top of the line laptop or computer in order to run a majority of the available trading software. You do, however, need to have something that exceeds the minimum required specifications if you want to avoid crashes or lag at the worst possible moments. Primarily, this means you are going to want to have plenty of available ram to allow you to multitask as needed. As you develop a need for more advanced software, your hardware needs are going to increase as well. While these costs can really add up when new hardware is purchased all at once, this is rarely necessary. Instead you can purchase parts piecemeal overtime and grow your hardware's capabilities as your skill as a day trader improves.

Once you really get serious, you are going to want to run at least two monitors at once in order to trade on one and do research and track results on the other. This, in turn, means that you will need a higher quality dedicated video card with space for multiple inputs as an integrated option just won't cut it. At this point, depending on your system, you may need to look into liquid cooling options in order to ensure your system doesn't overheat in the middle of a major trade.

Additionally, you are going to want to invest in the highest available internet speed that you can find. Currently 1 gigabyte speeds are available in major markets, while something around 100 mbps is plenty fast for most systems. While having access to that speed is all well and good, it is important that you have a modem and router that can keep up as they will be the major bottleneck in this scenario. While you are in contact with your internet service provider, you are likely going to want to consider reinstalling a landline as well, just in case you find yourself unable to complete a trade in any other way. Having a hardline to your brokerage can be the difference between success and failure of a major trade, more than worth the $10 a month a phone line costs these days.

Brokerage: Many traders choose their first online brokerage when they are first getting started in trading and never think about their choice again. This is a big mistake, however, because an advanced trader's needs are very different from those of a beginner. As such, once you have some trading experience under your belt it is important to reevaluate your previous choice to determine if you truly made a good decision. First things first, in order to see what your available options are, you are going to want to visit the forums of your favorite day trading website and see what other traders have to say.

Once you have a suitable list, the next thing that you are going to want to consider is the fees that each offers, as well as any fringe benefits they provide. If you already have a trading platform and other online tools that you have a strong preference for, take special care to consider other brokerages who support them or you risk having to learn the ins and outs of new software from scratch. It is also important to choose an online brokerage from your home country or, barring that, one that operates somewhere that provides proper oversight for such things. While some foreign brokerages might have cheaper fees, putting your money in the hands of a company without the right oversight puts you at risk of losing your trading capital every single day.

Last but not least, you are going to want to see what type of customer service the brokerages that stand out to you provide. When it comes to customer service, you aren't going to want to listen to reviews, it is best to see for yourself. To do so, you are going to want to call the brokerage in question and see how long it takes you to get in touch with a real person. While this won't often be a necessity, if you have to call your brokerage it is likely an emergency and you will want to know that someone is waiting on the other end of the line.

As a new potential customer, you may need to expect a call back from the brokerage. If they don't get back to you with 24 hours, move on. If the brokerage treats new potential customers with such disdain, consider how they are likely to respond once they already have your money. Assuming their live support is up to par, you should then try emailing the brokerage with a few questions and see how quickly they respond as this will likely be your primary mode of contact in the future. While this can be time consuming, customer service is what separates the best brokerages from the pack and its importance cannot be over emphasized.

Day trading tools online: There is no shortage of available online tools when it comes to helping you maximize your day trading efficiency. The first thing you will want to find is a financial calendar that meets your needs. Ideally, this will provide a collection of importance events, a variety of customizable dates and also details on several different markets. If you dabble in the forex market you will also want a currency convertor that shows the changes to various currencies in real time as well as convertor that displays the range a pair of currency have inhabited over a definable period of time.

You should also find a calculator that will help determine pivot points as well as relevant Fibonacci numbers. These tools allow you to keep up to date on meaningful trends, keeping you in the know when it comes to important details that are easy to miss otherwise. Similarly, you also want to find a heat map that you trust to show you trades that are currently popular and a volatility monitor so you can keep tabs on the mood of the market.

Platforms to consider

These days there are so many different trading platforms that finding the right one can be needlessly complex. The list below helps to simplify things somewhat by gathering together those that are most popular at the moment. This doesn't mean you shouldn't do your own research if there is something specific you are looking for it is only to help point you in the right direction.

OptionsHouse.com: This is a low frills trading platform that is perfect for those who just want to focus on trading. It offers a suite of modifiable tools, no minimum account balance and a flat commission rate of $4.95 for each trade.

InteractiveBrokers.com: At the other end of the spectrum, this site requires $10,000 up front, though the requirements aren't as steep if you are under the age of 25. They take $.005 from each traded share and also offer a vast option base include forex, precious metals, futures and more.

Ameritrade.com: Frequently referred to as the best trading platform on the market today, this site charges a flat fee of $9.99 per trade. They off a low required balance, multiple internal trading platforms and access to curated research. Alternately, they also offer a secondary platform called Trade Architect which is ideal for those who are looking for a simple and straightforward platform.

TradeStation.com: This site boasts of its fast order execution and charges a varying commission on trades that is somewhere between $5 and $10 based on the volume of the trade. They also require a $5,000 minimum account balance and a $99 monthly fee though this is waved with a large enough monthly trade volume. Their trade platform is also renowned for being quite robust.

Trade software

Day trading software is evolving practically at the speed the market changes. As such, if you hope to maintain the greatest advantage possible it is important to update the software you use on a regular basis. The options below are some of the most commonly used software on the market today.

eSignal: This software includes a highly rated mobile application along with charting and analyzing capabilities said to be the best in its class. Additionally, it provides multiple alternatives for charting and scanning both individual and groups of stocks. They also provide a wealth of customizable chart options when it comes to indicators including momentum MACD, distribution, volume, accumulation and more. If you are looking to continue your day trading education they also offer trading education seminars, newsletters and forums.

Multichart: If you are looking for a way to view as many up to the minute data streams as possible, this is the software for you. Once you find the streams you are looking for it also allows you to create charts with data from numerous sources. The options for charting are vast as well; including, drawing, 3D charting, back testing and several strategy and management options. What's more, it allows you to choose a pricing plan based on the tools you plan to use.

NinjaTrader: This easy to use and affordable software is a great place to start if you are just starting to use more advanced day trading software. It features a simple and intuitive charting function that doesn't sacrifice anything when it comes to power or stat tracking. It provides users the ability to track executions and account positions and even trade automatically. It also allows users to scan the market in real time according to predetermined criteria.

Trade-Ideas: Knowing how to pick the few stocks that are going to move in a given day is a crucial part of day trading successfully. The best way to do so is via a stock scanning software and the best stock scanning software on the market is from Trade-Ideas. It includes loads of predefined searches including biggest gainers/losers, turbo breaks, volume spikes, HOD movers plus hundreds of different custom filters to ensure you can easily find what it is you are looking for whatever it may be.

CHAPTER 5: TRADING STRATEGY: MODIFIED BUTTERFLY SPREAD

 When trading options, many day traders content themselves with utilizing calls and puts to make a profit from market decision or maybe using covered calls to generate income. There are more promising alternatives out there, however, one of which is the butterfly spread. The butterfly spread allows knowledgeable traders to pinpoint trades that are likely to generate a greater amount of profit for a limited amount of risk. The modified butterfly spread, discussed below, takes things a step further.

Modified spread compared to traditional spread

Standard butterfly: To understand what sets the modified butterfly spread apart, a look at the standard butterfly may be helpful. To perform the basic butterfly spread you utilize three calls or puts in a 1/2/1 configuration. The first call is purchased at a strike price comparable to the price of the underlying asset, another pair is purchased at a great price and a third is purchased at a price that is greater still. If dealing in puts, the strike prices descend in order instead.

The end result is a neutral trade that will generate a profit as long as the underlying asset stays within the range of the three strike prices. It is also useful when it comes to making directional trades by setting all of the strike prices above or below the current price. When utilized properly, this strategy ensures a low and well-defined level of risk with a reliable potential for profit and a relatively high chance of generating a significant rate of return.

Modified butterfly spread: The advanced form of this strategy has similar goals but differs from the simple version in a few key ways. Most importantly, it provides the user the opportunity to ensure that put trades are bullish and call trades are bearish. This occurs through the use of a 1/3/2 ratio which leaves just one price point where breaking even occurs. This, in turn, provides a sort of cushion that will allow you more leeway than the simple alternative.

As an example, assume an underlying asset is currently going for $194 a share. To execute the modified butterfly, you would then purchase a put at $194.50, sell three more at $190 and then buy a final pair at $175. The key takeaway here is the puts that are selling at 5 points below the at-the-money point and the second pair that are 20 points below. While the current price is $194 this means you can break even if the price dips down to roughly $184 which means the strategy generated roughly 5 percent of downside protection points.

This, in turn, mean that the underlying asset would need to drop more than 5 percent before a loss would occur. The total amount of available risk in this scenario is roughly $2,000 which equates with the amount required to facilitate the trade. This loss amount would not come into play until the underlying asset dropped below $175. On the other hand, the amount of possible profit in this example would be roughly $1,000 which equates to approximately a 50 percent return on the initial investment assuming the underlying asset increases to $200. The strategy would also result in a $500 profit as long as the underlying asset doesn't move past $195.

While the modified butterfly spread is riskier than the traditional version, it also has a greater profit to risk ratio. The most common timeframe given for a modified butterfly spread is six weeks. It is an ideal strategy to use if you believe the underlying asset is going to remain mostly stable over the timeframe you have chosen. It is the perfect choice if you are hoping for capital gains on an underlying asset that is likely to remain in the middle of the road.

Important criteria

When determining the type of butterfly spread to use, it is important to be aware of the amount of capital you are willing to risk. You will also want to know the estimated return that risk will generate and the likelihood of success and failure. There is no right answer to these criteria, you will need to set your own limits in order to determine which type of butterfly spread is right for you.

The potential rate of return, along with the likelihood of it being generated are going to directly determine the amount of risk it is in your interest to move forward on. Performing your own risk/reward analysis is crucial in this instance and it is important to not rush into modified butterfly spread just for the purpose of mixing things up. Regardless, it is recommended that you only attempt the modified version if you have a sizeable amount of trade capital backing you up.

Options trading are ideal for day traders who are interested in maximizing their potential for flexibility which can help nullify a risk/reward ratio that is not as strong as you might like. As long as you use it sparingly, and in the right conditions, the modified butterfly spread is a useful way of maximizing this flexibility even more.

CHAPTER 6: TRADING STRATEGY: VALUE AREAS AND ORDER FLOW SEQUENCING

Order flow sequencing is a useful strategy that was developed by a trader who spent time at both Bear Stearns and Sungard Capital Markets before striking out on his own. The goal here is to document and track relevant prices as they apply to the movements of the major players in a given market to determine what they are likely to do next and when they are likely to start. This then, allows traders in the know to more easily identify points of greater liquidity along with greater risks with a level of transparency which can be applied to the market as a whole.

Order flow sequencing first gained popularity during the early years of the last century when market generated information first started to be a requirement for successful daily trading. When compared to other indicator based analysis methods, it works much more quickly while also focusing on the present instead of the past. This, in turn, means that when used properly you still have time to put the results into action.

When it comes to considering the major players in your market of choice, you may find it helpful to think of them in the way you would the House when it comes to casino gambling. Eventually the House will always win when given a long enough time frame. Major players have the same advantage and you will almost always find it harder to make money when trading against them instead of with them. Instead, it is much easier to travel in their wake and pick up the scraps from their big money trades. Depending on the market in question, major players include financial institutions, traditional banks, hedge funds, commercial traders, and even governments. You know you are on the right track if the entity you are following can make waves in your chosen market just by executing a single trade.

Understanding the trends that these entities generate will make it much easier for you to recognize and track potential advantageous movements based on order flow techniques. This results in a clear indication of the disruption that the major players leave in their wake. Tracking these disruptions will then make it much easier for you to be on the winning side the next time it happens.

Additionally, using order flow sequencing you will find that it is much easier to understand the how's and whys of price fluctuation in your chosen market.

Value areas

In order to use order flow sequencing effectively, the first thing you need to understand is the concept of value areas. Determining the value area is the best way to determine when any relevant major players are likely to make a move and what that move will be. Value areas can be broken down into three key parts, the high point, the low point, and the control point. High point value area levels are points where the volume and demand of a specific trade has left prices at an extremely expensive point. On the contrary, low point value areas are points where the price has dropped to a point that the major players are likely to come sniffing around. The control point value area is the point the price of the underlying asset is at when you do your analysis.

The easiest way to track the various value areas is through the use of a volume profile tool. This tool will let you compare historical volume levels to current levels over a predetermined period of time. All you need to do is then look for points of overlap between the past and the present. Comparing the control point to the previous high and low points will give you an idea of when the major players are likely to make a move. Ideally, you will want to find a control point that is near the historical low point. Points of confluence then indicate areas you should be interested in, though you won't want to consider them as they emerge. Utilizing this strategy on the fly is asking for trouble, it should primarily be used to plan ahead.

In this instance, volume is going to always be the simplest way to determine where the market is likely heading. If the volume is low then you can bet a shift is on the horizon. Remember, previous points of price rejection are the best places to start when determining where the next instance is going to occur. Keeping an eye on volume will also provide secondary confirmation as to when the major players are likely going to begin making purchases. Luckily, determining these guidelines is relatively straightforward, and depending on the results, can remain relevant for several weeks or longer with only minor tweaking.

Tracking sequences of order flow

After you are clear on the current relevant value areas, you will want to start tracking the general flow of orders as they come in. This will let you start to see the volume as it is created, giving you a window to prepare the proper entry and exit points. To put it another way, rather than looking at candlestick charts after the fact you can then watch the candlestick form. After you have established your value areas correctly is when being aware of order flow will truly start paying off.

At the start of each new day you are going to want to double check that any relevant value areas are still currently where you expect them to be. With that out of the way, it is a simple matter to find points where the volume will begin to dip while also pinpoint scenarios where price rejection will set in. Essentially, all you will need to do is discover the points where the high point and low point align with the volume levels you have already defined. This will give you likely entry and exit points.

While taking the time to determine all the details every single day might sound like a waste of time, it is important to consider the alternative. Specifically, all of your trades will end up being at the mercy of the major players in your chosen market. What's even worse, you won't know when you are working with incomplete information. If you find yourself making trades that are logical and follow your plan, but you still aren't seeing the results you like, then order flow sequencing may well be the missing piece of the puzzle.

Order flow tracking programs

There are several different order flow tracking programs available online these days. The following list of companies produce those that are currently the most popular, most effective and rated the highest in customer satisfaction

Jigsawtrading.com: Jigsaw tools allow for the

tracking of the stock, futures and forex markets as part of a standard suite of commonly used functions. They can track time and DOM sales along with several advanced features displayed in an intuitive fashion. Even better, their products are available for free for a limited time.

Ninjacators.com: The tools available at Ninjacators.com provide a greater access to customer settings while also allowing users to access every market for options in the world across every timetable you might expect. They are known for their unique split order flow tool which allows users to plot orders on both sides of a candle at once.

CHAPTER 7: TRADING STRATEGY: FOREX OPTIONS HEDGING

The forex market has a reputation of being one of the more difficult markets to regularly make a profit from. However, this is only because of short scammers and traders who expect to see large returns in a short period of time due to the way the market often worked at the turn of the century. In order to ensure that the risk reward ratio balances out, it is important to have a proper way to hedge your trades. When utilized correctly, forex hedging provides traders with the opportunity to protect themselves regardless if they are planning to go long or short on a specific currency pair.

There are two primary ways of hedging a forex trade. The first is through using what are known as spot contracts which can be ineffective as they are often considered a short-term solution. The more effective of the two is known as a forex option. As the name implies, these trades provide the buyer the option, not the obligation, to buy or sell a currency pair at a set price at some point in the future. This strategy can be combined with several other strategies including bull and bear spreads, long straddles and long strangles.

Determine the risk

There are three steps to determine if a forex hedging strategy is the right choice based around the amount of risk you care to expose yourself to. The forex market is inherently riskier than most other markets which is what makes this strategy so crucial to long term success.

Risk analysis: The first thing that you need to do in order to hedge a forex trade properly is determine the level of risk that is inherent in the given currency pair. To accurately determine this, you will need to consider the implications of both letting the trade proceed normally and hedging it. This risk depends on the market and will likely be either visibly low or visibly high, if it is in the middle then you should hold off until a clear direction can be determined.

Consider your acceptable level of risk: Once you know the likely level of risk for the trade in question, the next thing you will need to do is determine if the level of risk is worth the extra costs that will be incurred by hedging it. This is as easy as looking at the potential gains and comparing them to the added costs and should be fairly straightforward.

Decide how to move forward: With the facts in front of you, the next step is to choose the strategy that is the most logical in the moment, remember, numbers don't lie. Your focus should be on the bottom line and the strategy that will generate the greatest return for your investment.

Forex hedging strategies

A good rule of thumb is the longer the term of any put options you use, and the lower the strike price, the more reliable the hedging strategy is going to be. While the initial cost is going to be significantly higher than not using a hedging strategy, the longer it stays in place the more cost effective it becomes. This makes it a particularly effective go-to when you are considering long term strategies. It is also much more cost effective to hedge indices as opposed to individual currency pairs.

You will also want to be aware that hedging will mitigate risk related to a dramatic change in value, but is ineffective when it comes to countering the risk that comes from general underperformance, something that will only be clear in the long term. This means it is really only worthwhile for risky trades that promise large payoffs. Additionally, you will need to keep in mind that not all forex brokers allow hedging so it is worth looking into before you mentally commit to anything.

Time extensions and put rolling: An excellent way to maximize the value of a hedge is to make a point of always choosing the put option with the greatest amount of available lead time. This is simply a matter of cost/benefit analysis as one option that lasts for six months is going to be much less expensive than two three month options. The ultimate marginal cost of maximizing your option provides you with the least expensive form of daily trade protection possible.

This is useful as you can turn a six-month option into a twelve-month option while still keeping the same strike price. This is known as rolling and it will let you take advantage of market changes as they appear. Assuming you have a strike price that is below the average market value you can keep an option rolling for years with only a minimal extra cost. This is exceptionally useful if you combine it with a highly leveraged investment that promises a large return as it mitigates a large amount of the potential risk.

Calendar spread: A calendar spread is created when both a long and short-term put option are bought and sold using the same strike price. The goal with this strategy is to let the shorter of the two puts expire at the end of its timeframe while letting the longer put serve as a hedge for future movement. When properly implemented, a calendar spread can generate a surprisingly cheap and effective hedge that can then be maintained indefinitely. It is important to consider the market prospects in the extreme long term before committing to this strategy as it can easily open you up to a significantly increased amount of total risk especially when it comes to underperformance.

CHAPTER 8: TRADING STRATEGY: SCALPING BOLLINGER STRATEGY

Forex scalping is commonly used in conjunction with short-term options in order to guarantee a profit. It works by opening and closing positions quickly in order to maximize the number of short, somewhat profitable, trades per day. When used properly you will hold on to individual positions for as little as a minute at a time. Many traders enjoy the Bollinger band scalping system because it is easy to accumulate profits in a short period of time in a fairly straightforward way. On the flipside, however, the sheer number of trades opens you up to increased risk when compared with the potential reward.

With that in mind, expert Bollinger band traders tend to accumulate gains faster than practically any other type of trader. If you already understand the basics of scalping and are looking for a way to maximize your profits in the forex market then choosing this strategy may be a no-brainer.

Bollinger band strategy 1

Strategy basics: This system revolves around an Exponential Moving Average along with a pair of Bollinger bands and is useful with virtually all currency pairs and time frames. With that being said, the most common and effective timeframe tends to be 5 minutes. Bollinger bands are a type of technical indicator which default to twenty periods with a standard deviation of two. However, with this strategy you want to set one band to twenty-one periods with a standard deviation of two and the other to twenty-one periods and a standard deviation of three.

The end goal here is to locate periods when the price touches a point that is between the pair of standard deviations. Once this occurs you will want to use a moving average of 200 as the guideline that allows you to accurately monitor the trend. If the price rises above the 200 point, then you can profit from long positions and if it drops then you can profit from short positions. At the same time, you will want to keep an eye out for a candle to form and close inside the space between the two deviations. If the opposite occurs then it indicates a reversal.

Parsing the data: When the conditions outlined above are met, then you know that you can open a trade at the start of the next candle with minimal risk. You will want to place a stop-loss either above or below the candles depending on the type of trade you are making. You may also want to set the target at the average of the pair of Bollinger bands with a second target set at either the upper or lower line, depending on the type of trade you are considering. This system has proven effective in virtually all situations as long as you take into account the price as it relates to the moving average of 200. This is a somewhat complicated strategy to put into practice, so making a few low-impact trades with it is recommended before moving to the big time.

Bollinger band strategy 2

This strategy is only effective with the GBP/USD and EUR/USD currency pairs in the 5-minute range. It is most effective when used in a market that is currently range bound with Bollinger bands that appear nearly flat. To use this strategy properly you will want to set the period of the bands to twenty with a standard deviation of two. It can work as expected during both the European and US trading sessions.

In order to use this strategy effectively you will want to buy when the bands are practically flat and the current price touches the lower of the two. You will then want to set a stop-loss that is 10 pips below the initial starting price. You will want to close out the trade once the price reaches the higher of the bands. If you are selling then you will want to do so when the price touches the top band and set a stop-loss that is 10 pips above the starting price. You will then close out the trade when the price reaches the lower of the two bands. This strategy can be more complicated than it first appears and practicing before putting into action is recommended.

One hour strategy

While not quite as short as the others, the goal of this strategy is to always make 50 pips with each trade. This system is proven effective in any trading session and works with pairs GBP/USD, EUR/USD, USD/JPY, NZD/USD, AUD/USD and USD/CAD. It will be most effective in a market environment that is range bound and features a pair of Bollinger bands that are virtually flat.

When buying and selling, if the current trend appears bullish, or the price touches the top band, you will want to generate an order with a stop-loss that is 35 pips below the starting price or at the previous low point, whichever is higher. Additionally, you will want to sell if the price rises 50 pips. You will also want to sell if the trend turns bearish or the price touches the lower of the bands. If you want to generate a sell order then you will use the same details as if the trend was bullish. As with the other strategies, practicing first is recommended as it is more complicated than it may first appear.

Extreme scalping

This system requires Bollinger bands that are set to twenty-one periods with a standard deviation of two. It is useful for timetables of one minute that have an RSI of fourteen, seventy, thirty. The goal here is to wait for the price to rise above one of the Bollinger bands while at the same time have the RSI increase to above seventy or to below thirty. The ideal target in this case is the dead center of the pair of bands with a pair of stop-loss five to seven pips higher and lower. As with the other strategies, practicing is recommended as it is more complicated than it may first appear.

CHAPTER 9: TRADING STRATEGY: FUTURES SPREAD TRADING

While it requires a firm grasp of the complexities of the futures market, futures spread trading offers great rewards for those brave enough to utilize it. As such, it is often seen as the realm of the true professional and something every day trader should one day aspire to.

Common spread types: commodity futures

Inter-commodity futures: These futures involve contracts that are spread across various markets. As an example, if you believe that the wheat market is going to experience a high demand when compared to the corn market then you would buy wheat and sell corn. The specific prices for each don't matter as long as wheat prices beat corn prices.

Calendar Intra-Commodity: This spread looks at a single commodity between differing months of the year. As an example, if you believe that the wheat market is going to be stronger in November as opposed to June then you would go long in November and short in June. The specifics of the price don't matter as long as prices are higher in November than they are in June.

Bull futures: This spread looks at a single commodity under the assumption that the sooner month will boast a higher price than the later month. As an example, if you buy a bullish wheat future in May then you will want the price to be higher then, than when you sell it in June. For this type of future, it is important to keep in mind that near future contracts tend to move faster the further you get from the front month which gives this future its name. A bullish trader would then be one who buys in the front month in hope that it ends up moving at a greater rate than the deferred month.

Bear futures: This spread occurs if you purchase the same commodity in such a way that you are short in the front month and long on the deferred month. As an example, if you purchase wheat in May and sell it in June then you are hoping the prices are lower in May than they will be in June. For this type of future, it is important to keep in mind that near future contracts tend to move faster the further you get from the front month which gives this future its name. If you are confident that prices are at a low point then this is the type of spread you should consider buying into.

Futures spreads trading margins

It is important to keep in mind that if they are part of a spread then the individual margins on specific contracts are going to be reduced. As an example, if the margin on a specific wheat contract alone is $2,000, but if you go both long and short on wheat in the same year then the margin between the pair could be as little as $200. If you go both long and short on the same commodity in different years the margin will be roughly double, so in this case it would be about $400. The price differential occurs because the volatility of the spread is lower than that of the individual contract.

Essentially, the futures spread provides you with the ability to consider the market in slow motion. As such, if something serious happened in the wheat market then both contracts would be affected in the same way which provides a level of protection against the increased risk that the single contract doesn't have.

Futures spread pricing

The price of a futures spread can be determined by the perceived difference in the two contracts. To determine what the spread's pricing is going to be, all you need to do is subtract the deferred month price from the front month price. If the front month price is lower, the spread will be negative while if it is higher the spread will be positive. The tick values for both spreads and individual contracts are going to remain the same. As an example, if the price of wheat in June was $500 per bushel and in July it is $510 then the spread price is -$10. Meanwhile if the difference was $500 and $490 then the spread would be $10.

Types of markets

Contango markets: A market is considered Contango if the front month is obviously going to have a lower cost than the deferred month. Typically, this means the deferred month is going to cost slightly more than the front month due to cost to carry. The cost to carry takes into account the interest rate on the capital that is related to operating and owning the store that actually sells the commodity along with storage costs for keeping the commodity for the extra time along with additional insurance costs. This is considered the default type of market.

Backwardation markets: A market is thought to be in backwardation if the near months are valued highly when compared to the deferred months. Also known as an inverted market, it is the opposite of the standard market condition. It most commonly occurs if the market is in the midst of a bull phase which is often caused by an issue with the supply chain or a dramatic increase in demand coupled with a limited supply. The price differential occurs because the front months are going to feel the full brunt of the situation while it is more likely to be mitigated by the time the deferred months arrive. This is even more likely to be the case if the deferred month is in a different crop year from the front month.

Regardless of the current state of the market it is important to take seasonal concerns into account as well. Generally, gasoline prices are always going to be higher in the summer and the prices of heating oil, natural gas, and coffee are always going to be higher in the winter. Additionally, it is important to keep in mind that while all markets experience bullish and bearish periods, those experienced by the commodities are less consistent.

CONCLUSION

Thank you for making it through to the end of *Day Trading: The Ultimate Guide to Day Trading*, let's hope it was informative and able to provide you with all of the tools you need to achieve your financial goals, whatever it is that they may be. Just because you've finished this book doesn't mean there is nothing left to learn on the topic, expanding your horizons is the only way to find the mastery you seek.

The next step is to stop reading already and start preparing yourself to ensure that you are ready to do everything in your power in order to ensure that the time you spend trading is as profitable as it can possibly be. Armed with the tips, tricks, and strategies in the preceding chapters you will soon find that you can maximize your dedication and hard work to successfully conquer even the highest risk trades and claim the largest rewards.

That is not to say that major windfalls are going to come along every day, however. Just because you are ready to handle what day trading throws at you doesn't mean that you won't experience losses, and a great deal of them besides. Whatever you do, always keep in mind that crafting a trading plan that is sixty-five percent successful is considered extremely impressive. Only by keeping your expectations in check can you be sure that your emotions don't get the better of you and that you can survive day trading in the long term.

No matter how the minute to minute excitement makes you feel, it is always going to be more important to do your homework and faithfully execute on your plan no matter what, only then will you find the profits you seek. Don't forget, day trading is a marathon, not a sprint, slow and steady wins the race.

OPTIONS TRADING: THE ULTIMATE GUIDE TO OPTIONS TRADING: UNCOVERING OPTIONS TRADING PROFIT MAKING SECRETS

DESCRIPTION

If you have ever spent any real time trading in one or more of the asset investment markets, then you know how little freedom you sometimes have to go your own way and set your parameters for financial success as they make sense to you. Not so with options trading, which, as the name implies provides you with the option, not the obligation to carry through on what you have started. What's more based on the state of the market at the moment, you can easily transfer all of your existing skill into this new way of trading without missing a beat. If you are already somewhat familiar with options trading but want to take your skills to the next level then *Options Trading: The Ultimate Guide to Options Trading* is the book you have been waiting for.

Studies show that barely more than 10 percent of all options traders display the type of mindset that will help them be successful in the long term. Inside you will learn not just what it takes to form the type of mindset that will lead you to success, you will also learn important tips that the best options traders utilize on a daily basis along with the mistakes that many traders of all skill levels fall into and how you can avoid them for yourself. You will also learn what a reliable options trading plan looks like and how to measure the metrics of your current system to ensure that it measures up.

When it comes to being successful in the options trading market, it is all about the strategies that you use which is why inside you will find more than a dozen different strategies that are proven effective. You will find strategies that you will use every day as well as those which are going to be useful in more specialized situations. No matter your skill level or experience, *Options Trading: The Ultimate Guide to Options Trading* has something you can use.

If you know that you have it in you to be successful in the asset market, but you haven't quite found the right niche, then what are you waiting for? Take control of your financial future and buy this book today!

Inside you will find

- The difference between liquid and illiquid options and which you stay away from more often than not.
- Why it is important to consider historical volatility before you make any moves.
- Which metrics you are going to want to consider in order to determine if your trading plan is a dud or a financial stud.

- Ten different trading strategies for all seasons and market moods and how to get the most out of each one.
- Several specialized and advanced trading techniques and when to use them for maximum profit.
- *And more...*

INTRODUCTION

Congratulations on downloading *Options Trading: The Ultimate Guide to Options Trading* and thank you for doing so. When it comes to jumping into investment trading, options are easier than many other choices only because they rely more on existing knowledge of the underlying asset markets. This doesn't mean it is a straightforward process, however, and if you aren't careful, you can lose the sum total of your trading capital just as quickly as anywhere else.

To help ensure you are as successful as possible, the following chapters will discuss everything you need to know in order to ensure your time spent trading options is as easy and fruitful as possible. First, you will learn all about the mindset you need to adopt if you are going to be successful at options trading, not just in the short term but for the long term as well. From there you will learn many of the essential tips for success that experienced options traders use every day as well as the mistakes that many traders of all skill levels fall into and how you can avoid them for yourself. You will also learn about the importance of analyzing your trades and how to make sure that your trading system or plan is as efficient as possible. Finally, you will learn all about the many different trading strategies that you will use on a regular basis as well as several more specific trading strategies that can lead to major profits if utilized successfully. When you are finished there will be no option, no matter how convoluted that can stand in your way.

There are plenty of books on this subject on the market, thanks again for choosing this one! Every effort was made to ensure it is full of as much useful information as possible, please enjoy!

CHAPTER 1: THE MINDSET OF THE SUCCESSFUL OPTIONS TRADER

Studies show that barely more than 10 percent of all options traders display the type of mindset that will help them be successful in the long term. If you ever hope to be one of them, the first thing you need to do is to separate your emotions from your actions. Instead of letting your emotions factor into your trading strategy you need to remove them from the equation entirely by striving for the purely logical mindset that the best options traders cultivate. Following the suggestions outlined below will allow you to focus on long-term success regardless of what distractions are currently taking place around you, naturally improve your successful trade ratio in the process.

Have the right expectations: When it comes to honing your trader's mindset, perhaps the most important thing you can do is understand the results you are likely to experience. Having realistic expectations will allow you to respond appropriately both in times of failure as well as success. Specifically, this means you are going to want to banish thoughts of major success in a short period of time. This, in turn, will make it easier for you to prevent negative thoughts from creeping in throughout the day and causing you to take risks you otherwise would not take.

Additionally, it is important to be aware of what your emotional triggers are while trading. As everyone's triggers are different, the best way to understand your own is to keep a trading journal. In this journal, you are going to want to keep track of all of your trades, both successful and unsuccessful. You are going to want to note the date of each trade, the specifics surrounding it, the emotions you felt at the time, whether or not it was successful and why.

This exercise will not only help you to be aware of the emotions you are likely to experience in the future; it will help you understand why they appear in the first place. Emotions are the enemy of good trades and the best way to outpace your enemy is to know them inside and out.

For many traders, the strongest emotional triggers occur because they believe that correctly executing on a plan should lead to success 100 percent of the time. This stems from a misunderstanding of what considering a plan successful actually means. When it comes to options trading, a successful plan is one that hovers around a 60 percent success rate. This means that the scheme is extremely likely to turn a profit in the long run but a full 40 percent of the time it is used it will end in failure.

Losses are an unavoidable part of the investment process as risk is what ultimately leads to profit. If every investment were a guaranteed success, no one would bet against it, and there would be no chance for a profit. To mitigate these feelings, it is important to understand that a good trade is not one that made money but rather one that followed your system to the letter. In order to do so properly, you need to focus exclusively on your long-term results and treat everything else as meaningless noise.

This means you will want to wait at least a month between periods where you update your plan as anything less isn't going to provide you with enough details to make changes effectively. A significant moment in your evolution as an options trader will be the moment you can see why the trader who struck it rich after a few random trades is less successful than a trader with a few different plans that are always executed on properly no matter what. Remember, an effective trader is a selective trader.

Additionally, it is important to view options trading as a marathon rather than a sprint. With this fact in mind, it will be much easier for you to consider unsuccessful trades as a learning experience rather than an abject failure. This will then make it easier to keep emotions out of the equation, a feat that will become even easier with practice.

Understand that sometimes it is okay to do nothing: Another negative mindset that many traders foster hinges on the idea that they always need to be trading. The reality is that inaction can be just as profitable as an extended trading day if the conditions are right. As long as you are not the writer of an option then creating a pull or call doesn't force you to take any specific action if things don't work out in your favor. This fact may seem obvious, but when thought about logically, it becomes difficult to put theory into practice when there is money on the line.

This is why it is important to include situations where not going through with a trade is the right choice in the system that you decide to use. Once again, as long as you listen to the system that you created when your mindset was at its best you have the potential to become an expert options trader.

One of the most important things you need to wean out of your trading habits is jumping into trades without thinking them through entirely. Getting into the habit of picking and choosing the best trades for your system will help you become a professional when it comes to separating the wheat from the chaff. Knowing how to do this will contribute to ensuring that you are not just getting lucky now and then when it comes to making trades.

The same goes for getting out of a trade that turned sour as sticking with it and hoping things turn around is on of the easiest ways to lose your shirt. The best choice is always going to be letting the trade in question speak for itself and, if the trade doesn't go the way you expect, use that as an opportunity to learn for next time.

Put more value on patience: Patience is one of the most important, and most difficult, thing for many traders to learn. This is because sitting idly by with money on the table is such a difficult skill to master. Luckily, like all skills, it can be improved with practice. In order to perfect this skill, it is important to internalize the fact that the market isn't always making big moves, even at times of peak volatility. A useful way of helping yourself learn patience is by never focusing on just one trade at a time. Keeping your options open makes it easier to put each trade in perspective and prevent any one trade from artificially inflating its importance in your mind.

This is not to say that individual trades should be treated flippantly. Rather, you need to consider each trade in a perspective that takes the entirety of your goal into account. Additionally, this means that you are going to want to come to terms with the fact that there will be some days where there just isn't much going on. Overtrading can be just as damaging to your bottom line as not trading enough or making bad trades, especially if your transaction fees are higher than you might prefer.

To help cultivate the right mindset you are going to want to set either monthly or weekly profit goals as opposed to daily trading goals. Setting daily goals will likely cause you to make erratic trades at the end of the day as you strive to meet your goal. Even if you do end up making the target amount each day to hit your goal, it is likely that at least some of these trades will not have stood up to the strict level of scrutiny that a good plan requires. What's worse, if you end up seeing results based on the poorly thought out trades then it can promote the formation of destructive habits moving forward.

It is important to focus on building the type of discipline that will serve you well in the long term as early in your trading career as possible as you will less be less likely to have major trades on the line. The longer you go without giving into your impulses, the easier it will be to ignore them completely.

Learn to adapt: While it is important to stick to your system when your emotions are telling you otherwise, it is equally important to understand that sometimes market situations will change on the fly. When this occurs, you are going to need to go off the book if you hope to see your current trade end in profit. At first, it is going to be difficult to determine when it is the right time to toe the line and when it is the right time to experiment as the only clear indicator is practice.

In order to ensure that you have to fly blind as infrequently as possible, you are going to want to have several different trading plans on hand that is ideal for different market states. Learning which plan is right for which situation and when it is time for a change, in real time, will help you see much greater overall returns a much greater portion of the time.

Regardless of your planning, sometimes the unexpected will occur which means that you will need to make a leap of faith in order to be successful. A competent trader will be aware of market signs that change is on the horizon and will be able to act accordingly. This is another skill that cannot be taught; it can only be gained by experience.

As long as you keep the appropriate mindset regarding individual trades, any new strategy that is attempted will result in valuable data, if nothing else. It is important to understand that learning not to use a specific course of action a second time is always valuable, no matter the costs. Working to build this into your core trading mindset will lead you to greater success in a wider variety of situations in the long term.

Put consistency above all else: When it comes to developing a professional trading mindset, you are going to need to learn to prioritize consistency in all things. This can be another fact that is easy to understand in theory but much more difficult to put into practice. In order to get to this point, you will need to deal with financial setbacks and profits that were less than they first appeared. Ensuring these types of situations don't happen in the future requires a level of inquisitiveness that isn't innate for many traders. Making a habit of digging deeper into the reasons behind your successes as well as your failures is sure to lead to a greater level of success overall.

While certain types of investment market trading lend themselves to high risk/high reward strategies, trading options is not one of them. The best options traders tend to prioritize reliable gains of middling size and leave the riskier trades to the novices. While a larger than average return is nothing to sneeze at, a reliable trading record is going to generate a greater level of gain in the long term.

Understand your strengths and weaknesses: In order to find success in the long term, it is important that you understand where your trading strengths and weaknesses lie. Only by reaching this level of personal understanding will you ever be able to create a trading plan that builds on the one while minimizing the other. This is another reason it is so important to keep a trading journal as it will help to reveal tendencies that you tend to repeat that you might not otherwise be aware of.

Doing so will help you to become more aware of when you are letting emotions cloud your judgment as it will be clear when you made trades that you would not have made at the beginning of the day when your head was clear. With enough practice, you will then be able to head these emotions off at the pass and take a break instead of letting your successful trade percentage suffer.

Focus on keeping a clear mind, and you will find that not only is it easier to stick to your system but that you are able to determine the specific causes for success or failure found in each trade as well. Practice keeping this mindset during every trade, and you will see a greater percentage of successful trades sooner than you may expect.

CHAPTER 2: TIPS FOR SUCCESS

Avoid call options that are out of the money: While most investment markets focus on the trend of buying low and selling high, this approach doesn't work when it comes to options trading. Putting your money on out of the money call options often devolves into little more than gambling, and there are more effective ways of gambling that have much higher odds of success. Additionally, making these types of trades can make it difficult for you to understand why the trade failed to return a profit which makes the whole thing an exercise in futility.

To understand why out of the money call options are a poor choice it is important to keep in mind that when you purchase an option, you are saying not only that you know how the underlying asset is going to move but also when that move is going to occur. If you make a mistake when judging either, you are going to be out the premium you paid for the option along with the cost of the commission as well. What's worse, your funds will then be tied up until the option expires meaning you may miss out on a preferable alternative in the interim. Remember, in order to see a return on this type of trade the underlying asset of an option that is out of the money needs not only to increase, it also needs to reach all the way to the strike price.

Know when to use varying strategies: Options trading offers up a wide variety of different strategies to ensure you don't end up trying to fit square pegs into round holes. For example, buying on spread will sometimes be an excellent way to capitalize on various market conditions, but only if you are aware of the specifics beforehand. Not only will focusing on a single strategy cost you money in the long run, but it will also skew your results by calculating false losses that were not indicative of the strength of the system in question.

Know the spread: A long spread is made up of a pair of options that are similar in every way except one has a higher strike price than the other. The option with the higher cost is being purchased while the other is being sold. These options can be either puts or calls. Long spreads comprised of calls are bullish, and those comprised of puts are bearish.

Despite the fact that when the time lapse hurts one-half of the spread, it helps the other, spreads ultimately hurt your profit potential in most cases. This is because one-half of the pair is practically always going to expire unless the underlying asset is extremely volatile. With that being said, if you are interested in reliability above all else then they are still a good choice.

Always have a clear point of entry and exit: To trade in the options market successfully, it is important to always have a clear idea of the ideal entry and exit points you are going to utilize. Not only will doing so help to mitigate the influence that emotion might have on each trade, but it will also ensure that you remain in the black over the long term. While it can be difficult to exit a trade when there is still the potential of money on the table, it is important to keep in mind that the potential for loss is also ever present. Setting a reasonable exit point and sticking with it is going to generate a larger profit over a prolonged period of time, guaranteed.

Avoid doubling up: If you are in the middle of a trade that appears to be going well and it suddenly turns around apparently at random, it is only natural to want to do anything you can to save it. Unfortunately, the best option virtually every single time is going to be to cut your losses and move on. In this situation, it is important to keep in mind that options are derivatives which mean the price is likely to change, and 'doubling down' is likely only going to lead to a greater overall loss.

While doubling down might feel like the right move at the moment, if you take the time to consider the amount of related time decay you are dealing with it can help to clear your head. If you still can determine what the right course of action is going to be all you need to do is to take an extra moment to clear your head and consider what you would have done in this situation if you weren't already committed. Nine times out of 10 the correct decision is going to be just to cut your losses and move on.

Stay away from illiquid options: Illiquidity measures the speed at which a specific option can be either bought or sold without causing the price to shift noticeably. Liquidity, on the other hand, can be thought of as the chance that the second trade of a given underlying asset will take place at the same price as the first. The stock market tends to be more liquid than the options market simply because there are fewer options related to each individual stock. As a result, you are automatically 10 percent more likely to end up on the losing side of a trade if you choose to move forward with an illiquid option.

Be willing to buy back short options: While, in theory, it might seem like buying back short options at the last moment is the best choice, this practice is sure to hurt you more than help you in the long run. It may be tempting to hold onto profitable options in order to squeeze the maximum return out of each investment, but you need to be aware that the potential for a reversal is always lurking in the shadows. Instead, a good rule of thumb is to buy back options that are currently at 80 percent of your ideal return or higher and let the extra take care of itself. While it may hurt to leave some potential profit on the table, it will improve your overall reliability, netting you a profit in the long run.

Keep earnings and dividend dates in mind: It is important to keep an eye on any underlying assets that you are currently working with as those who are currently holding calls have the potential to be assigned early dividends, with greater dividends having an increased chance of this occurrence. As owning an option doesn't mean owning the underlying asset, if this happens to you, then you won't be able to collect on your hard-earned money. The Early assignment is largely a random occurrence which means that if you don't keep your ear to the ground, it can be easy to get caught unaware and be unable to exercise the option before you miss the boat.

Along similar lines, you also want to be aware of when the earning season is going to take place for any of your underlying assets as it is likely going to increase the price of all of the contracts related to the underlying asset in question. Additionally, you will need to be caught up on current events as even the threat of influential news can be enough to cause a significant spike in volatility and premiums as well. In order to minimize the additional costs associated with trading during these periods, you are going to want to utilize a spread. Doing so will minimize the effect that inflation has on your bottom line.

Respond to an early assignment in the right way: When it comes time to sell the options you have purchased it is important to keep the possibility of early assignment in mind. To avoid unpleasantness, you are going to want to avoid lower-striking the long option in order to generate enough of the required underlying asset. Rather, you are going to want to place the long option onto the open market which will provide you with the chance to profit from the premium caused by the remaining time. You can then use your new funds to purchase the underlying asset that you are on the hook for, netting a profit in the process.

When you come up against an early assignment, it is important not to let your emotions get the better of you. Remember, the early assignment is more or less random so there is little you can do to prevent it from happening. Other traders aren't always going to make the best choices, and all you do is to roll with the punches. All you can do is to try and negate the chances of it affecting you as much as possible by being prepared for it depending on the mood of the market and its current level of volatility.

If you are going to utilize a spread, do it all at once: While purchasing a spread in a two-step process might seem like a good way to maximize profit, in reality, you are playing with fire. Specifically, purchasing a put or a call and then waiting to purchase the other half of the spread often leaves you open for the possibility of a reversal that will cost you more than what you would have made had things gone your way. Purchasing a spread as a single unit minimizes the number of variables that you have to contend with and increases your chance of success in the long term.

Take advantage of index options: Index options are a safe choice when the market is currently sporting a high degree of vulnerability. Index options are much less likely to experience sudden changes to a majority of news reports unless the results are extremely far reaching. The larger the index, the more likely it is that it will remain neutral.

On the other hand, if the market is in a holding pattern then you are going to want to consider short spreads on indices. In order to do so, you are going to want to choose an option pair with different strike prices in the standard fashion. This will largely remove time decay from the equation while also guaranteeing that you will make a profit as long as prices don't decrease.

Avoid making trades you cannot afford to lose: Regardless of how airtight your trading system appears to be, it is important to make it a habit of never investing more than you can afford to lose. No single trade is ever going to offer up enough of an incentive that taking the risk of knocking yourself out of the trading game entirely makes sense. Ensure that you know your limits beforehand for the absolute best results. In fact, a good rule of thumb is to never commit more than 2 percent of your total trading capital to any one trade. If you take this into account, then you would have to make 50 bad decisions in a row to lose all of your capital. If this occurs, you are likely focusing on the wrong investing and should consider your options carefully before continuing.

CHAPTER 3: MISTAKES TO AVOID

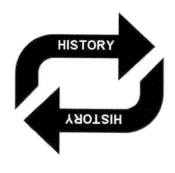

Not paying attention to the difference between implied volatility and historical volatility: When looking to trade successfully, implied volatility should be one of the primary ways to determine if a given option is priced correctly. Generally, the greater the amount of implied volatility, the more bearish the market will become and the more expensive most options sell for. However, historical volatility is just as important when it comes to choosing profitable options.

Historical volatility should also be determined beforehand so you can decide if the difference warrants further study. If this turns out to be the case, then you are going to want to take the time to go back at least 12 months with the underlying asset in the question in order to get a good baseline for the current state of things. While this can be time-consuming, it will ultimately be worthwhile if you find out things are not as they initially seemed.

Don't ignore probability: It is important to keep in mind that the historical data that you have access to will not apply to the current trend that the market is experiencing at all times. This means that to be successful, you are going to want to consider the probability as well as the odds that the market is going to behave expectedly. The probability is the ratio of the likelihood of a given outcome. Taking the time to understand the probability of a given outcome can make it easy to purchase the right options at the right time in order to minimize losses related to an underlying asset.

If you plan on purchasing cheap options, it is important to keep in mind that they are going to be cheap for a reason. The price is always determined by the strike price of the underlying asset combined with the amount of time remaining before the option expires. Cheap options are typically cheap because it is unlikely that they will turn a profit before they expire.

Don't ignore delta: If the delta of the option you are looking at is close to 1 then it is time to create calls, and if it is close to -1 then it is time to create puts. If you are dealing with especially cheap options, however, then it is important to look for options with a higher delta as they are more likely to behave in an expected fashion. This, in turn, allows you to expect greater gains when the underlying asset begins to move. Different strategies are going to require different levels of the delta to be successful. Never enter into a trade without knowing where the current delta stands and how it is likely to change in your chosen timeframe.

Avoid choosing the wrong parameters: If you are working with options that deal in front month contracts, then you are going to want to keep in mind the timeframe that relates to the expectations you have regarding the underlying asset in question. While some options are always going to look good on paper, it is important not to become enamored and risk buying into a timeframe that won't provide you with enough time to turn a profit. What's more, you are always going to want to maintain a realistic set of expectations when it comes to the way the underlying asset is going to move. If you choose poorly, then you can expect a wide range of fluctuation before the option in question expires.

Not using sentiment analysis: Sentiment analysis is easy to overlook which is unfortunate because it is a reliable way to determine the likelihood that a specific trend in an underlying asset is going to continue over a set timeframe. This means you are always going to want to observe instances of short interest as well as put activity and analyst ratings to get a fair idea of underlying stock price movement in the near term. When utilizing sentiment analysis, it can be easy to mistake actual results for the mood of the market. As such you are always going to want to wait for any initial gut reaction movement to clear up before making your move.

Not taking technical indicators into account: When working with cheap options, it is important to avoid making snap judgments as they are much harder to judge accurately compared those in the midrange. This is because cheap options that represent a likely sure thing are always picked up extremely quickly so what is left requires a deeper level of analysis in order to find the best deals. Using technical indicators can then help to ensure that whatever you do, it is likely to end in your favor.

Not looking at extrinsic and intrinsic value: The extrinsic value of an option is the difference between the current price it is listed at, compared with what you are guaranteed to make off its intrinsic value or the amount its premiums will pay out, even if it expires or there is no additional movement from the underlying asset. Everyone always takes into account the intrinsic value, but the extrinsic is often left out in the cold despite still being a useful indicator. While the intrinsic value is likely to stay the same, the extrinsic value is going to decrease as the option gets closer to expiring.

Not giving commission costs proper thought: Especially if you are interested in high risk/high reward trades, not giving enough thought to your commission costs can significantly impact your overall earnings. If you chose the brokerage that you are using early on in your trading career, then there may very well be a better option out there for you. Remember, not all brokerages are created equal which means that you may very well be able to find a much better rate with only a little bit of extra research.

If you are fairly certain that you won't be able to get a better rate than what you are currently working with, then it is important that you don't waste your trading potential by working for returns that will be dramatically reduced by the fees you pay. A good rule of thumb is that you should always try to at least triple what you are paying in commission fees on every successful trade. This will ensure that you have some wiggle room for failed trades without it negatively affecting your trading capital.

Not giving enough care to your stop losses: While it is known that you should always set a stop loss on options which have a large potential for success, or those that are extremely volatile, many traders still forgo this step when the stakes are lower. While not placing a stop loss on a relatively cheap option won't lose you much by itself, getting into this habit has the potential to cost you a great deal of time. Unless you get in the habit of always protecting yourself on every trade, every time, you run the risk of burning through your trading capital much faster than you otherwise might.

Avoid trying to adapt existing strategies: While it can be easy to come to think of a successful strategy as a safety blanket, trying to use one strategy in all situations is only asking for trouble. Every time you decide to change the type of options that you target, or note that the market is changing, you will find more success by starting from scratch on an entirely new strategy than trying to shoehorn in something that no longer works as effectively as it should. While this will ultimately lead to you trading less overall, your results are sure to speak for themselves.

CHAPTER 4: ANALYZING YOUR TRADES

In order to determine if your trading system is as effective as possible, it is important to keep track of your trades and analyze the results about once a month. It is important that you don't overanalyze your results as otherwise a handful of good (or bad) trades can throw the entire average off and cause you to move forward in a less than optimal manner.

The metrics that you are going to find to be the most helpful are going to vary based on your trading style. If you prefer high risk/high reward trades, then you are going to be more interested in total net profit while if you prefer to avoid as much risk as possible, then your successful trade percentage is going to be more useful. Regardless, it is vital that you review and thoroughly understand a wide variety of different performance metrics related to your plan or your system before determining if it is time to try something new.

Performance reports: A performance report for a strategy or trading plan is an overall measurement of how it performs at the top level. A good performance report will reflect on the rules you are trading by and compares the results to an overall historical context. Also known as backtesting, this is a useful process to perform either before you begin using a new plan or once you have already started if you feel that the way it has performed so far is a fluke. Most trading platforms can generate performance reports automatically both via back testing and in real time.

The first part of any performance report is the performance summary which outlines the most important metrics of the plan or system in question. It is common for these reports to include performance graphs, trade lists, and periodical returns. They keep track of every trade that you make, the time and date it occurred, the type of trade it was along with any profits or losses that resulted from it in the form of a percentage of the cost of the trade. Remember, keeping an eye on weekly data might not be especially helpful, though quarterly or monthly data will allow you to see the forest for the trees more easily.

This information is especially helpful when you want to know not just what your trading result totals are but why specific trades played out in a specific way. When studied properly they can easily allow you to see how individual flukes can be turned into patterns. They are also useful when it comes to ensuring that you don't repeat disastrous mistakes a second time.

These details can be found in the performance graph displayed as either a bar graph that shows a monthly net profit or through what is known as an equity curve. This graph is an excellent way of gaining an overall idea of the quality of trades that are made over a given period of time without dealing with the noise inherent in the market as a whole.

Metrics to consider

Every performance report is going to include a wealth of data, much more than you are going to need in most cases. This can make getting started difficult if you don't know where to look. Consider the following metrics first and then dig deeper if you still haven't found what you are looking for.

Total net profit: The total net profit broadly determines the success or failure of a plan or system over a specific period. This number can be found by taking the total gross loss, adding it to the commission costs, and then subtracting from the total amount made from successful trades. While it is good to know if you are turning a profit, the total net profit can be deceptive as well because it won't show how often your plan or system was successful, just the overall results.

Profit factor: In order to find the profit factor of your plan or system you will want to start with the total gross profits and then divide by the total gross losses with any relevant fees added in. If the result is greater than one, then you can consider your current strategy a success. This number equates to how many units of profit you can expect for every one unit of risk you undertake. The higher the number, the greater the difference between your wins and your losses.

Profitable percentage: Also known as the probability of winning, your profitable percentage can be found by taking the number of trades that you have made successfully and dividing it by the total number of trades that you have made overall. Unlike with profit factor, there is no right answer to this amount as it is going to vary based on personal trading style. If you prefer higher risk trades, then a smaller number is acceptable. If you prefer more reliable trades, then you want the number to be as high as possible.

Trade average net profit: The trade average net profit can be thought of as how reliable your system is overall, expressed in the amount of money that typically changed hands with each trade. To find this amount all you need to do is to divide the total profit you have made by the total number of trades. If the resulting number is negative, then you know your plan needs work. When figuring out the trade average net profit, you will want to leave out any exceptionally good or bad trades as they can easily skew the results.

CHAPTER 5: OPTION TRADING STRATEGIES TO CONSIDER

While throwing yourself whole hog into the options market means taking in a great deal of information in a short period of time, there are plenty of strategies to use that are likely to improve your returns and reduce your risk as greatly as possible.

Covered call: Also called the buy-write strategy, a covered call involves purchasing an underlying asset while also generating a call on the same asset. In order to ensure this strategy works properly, it is important to create a call based around how much of the underlying asset you own. This strategy is extremely effective if you own a separate position in the short term and feel that the underlying asset is either going to stay the same or decrease in value in the time frame for the option you created. When done properly, it allows you to generate a bonus premium at the very least. Covered calls are an effective strategy when used with index futures, LEAPS and on funds that are traded via an exchange and purchased on a margin.

Married puts: To utilize a married put, the first thing you need to do is purchase a specific amount of an underlying asset before purchasing a put that covers the same amount. This should be one of your go-to strategies if you feel bullish when it comes to the price of the asset in question and are looking for an easy way to minimize losses. The put that you purchased then acts as a price floor that can help prevent a dramatic drop in price. While putting money into an asset that you believe is going to decrease in price dramatically is never recommended, if you already own the underlying asset, then a married put will help minimize future uncertainty.

While a married put isn't going to be the right choice all of the time, when used sparingly under the right conditions it can be a reliable way to increase your overall success when it comes to options trading. To ensure that it always works out in your favor you are going to want to begin each transaction with a clear understanding of the risk in question. You can then factor in the added costs of a married put compared to the mitigation of that risk to determine if it is worth moving forward. As an added bonus, married puts help mitigate the potential risk related to early options to exercise as it ensures you always have available shares ready and waiting.

Bull call spread: To use this strategy, you will want to start by purchasing a call option at a strike price you believe to be beneficial. You will then want to sell a similar number of calls at a higher strike price. Both calls should have the same underlying asset and the same timeframe. This is a useful strategy to use if you are bullish on the strength of the underlying asset in question and your research indicates that the price is likely to increase in the time frame you have chosen.

This strategy is also known as a vertical credit spread because it has a pair of mismatched legs. Legs that are sold close to the money generate a credit spread that typically contains a net credit along with a positive time value. On the other hand, a debit spread is created with a short option that ends further from the money than when it started. Overall, this strategy is considered a net buy.

Bear put spread: The bear put spread is similar to the bull call spread but is used in opposite circumstances. Specifically, you begin by purchasing a pair of put options, one at a higher strike price and another at a lower strike price. You are going to want to purchase an equal number of each and ensure that they have the same underlying asset and timeframe. This strategy is useful when you feel bearish on the underlying asset in question as it helps you limit your losses if you are incorrect about the way the market is moving. This strategy should be used cautiously, however, as your overall profits are going to be limited to the difference between the two puts you purchased minus the cost of any transaction fees.

The ideal time to use a bear put spread is if you are interested in short selling an underlying asset and using a more common put option doesn't seem to be the right choice. You will find them useful if you are interested in speculating that prices are on a downward trend and don't want to invest a larger amount of capital waiting for the worst to happen. When using a bear put spread you are literally planning for the worst while hoping for the best.

Protective collar: To use the protective collar strategy you are going to want to start by purchasing a put option that is currently out of the money. You will then want to write a different call option based on the same underlying asset that is also out of the money. This is an ideal strategy to use when you have a long position on an underlying asset that has seen significant gains in the recent past. Using a protective collar allows you to both ensure the current level of profit while also holding onto the underlying asset in case it continues to increase in value.

Using a protective collar is as simple as placing the contract for the put option you purchased at a strike price that guarantees you hold on to a majority of the profit you have made. After that, you will be able to fund the collar strategy with the call option that you have written, making sure that it relates to a specific Digit. This strategy is a great way to maintain your profits while adding very little to your overall costs. What's more, it is very easy to ensure that you don't have to pay any related taxes as you can allow the option to roll over for as long as you deem necessary.

Straddles: The long straddle strategy is most useful after you have already purchased both a put and a call that share the same timeframe, underlying asset and strike price. It is useful if you believe that the price of the underlying asset is going to move significantly in one direction, you just don't know which direction it is going to be. Putting a long straddle into effect allows you to rest easy as you will see a gain as long as the price starts moving within the time frame you have chosen.

Alternatively, to institute a short straddle, you will want to sell a call and a put with the same timeframe, the same costs and related to the same underlying asset. This will ensure that you make a profit from the premium if you don't expect the underlying asset to move much in either direction in the specified timeframe. Be aware, however, that the odds of success will decrease proportionally to the amount that the underlying asset moves in the given timeframe.

Long strangle: In order to utilize a long strangle you will want to purchase both a put and a call that use the same underlying asset and share a maturation level. They are also going to need different strike prices. The strike price for the put should be somewhat lower than the price of the call, and both should be at a point out of the money. This is a useful strategy if you expect the underlying asset to move significantly but are unsure of the direction it will take. When used properly, you are virtually guaranteed a profit minus any related costs.

A strangle functions much like a straddle except that it tends to be cheaper as you are purchasing options that are already out of the money. This means you can routinely expect to pay as much as 50 percent less which makes it easier to play both sides of the fence. When given the option, a long strangle is preferable to a short straddle as it offers the chance at twice the premium while forcing you to take on the same amount of risk.

Butterfly spread: A butterfly spread requires the use of a bear spread strategy in addition to a bull strategy and contains three separate strike points. To start you want to purchase a call option at the lowest price you can manage. You will then want to sell two calls at a higher price and a third call at a price that is higher still. Your goal is to ensure a range of potential profits at prices you believe will be profitable. The most effective time to use a butterfly spread is when you have a neutral opinion on the current state of the market.

It is a good idea to utilize a butterfly spread when you expect the underlying asset that you favor to increase in price but are unsure of how much gain to expect. As such, you are going to want to make sure the overall market volatility is as low as possible. The higher the overall level of volatility, the more setting up a butterfly spread will cost you. The butterfly spread is not without a downside, however, as if you are wrong about the direction the underlying asset is going to move in then the losses can be significant.

Iron Condor: In order to use the iron condor strategy, you are going to want to start with a short position and a long position utilizing a pair of 'strangle' strategies to take full advantage of a market that is low in volatility. One 'strangle' is going to be long and the other short and set to an outer strike price. You can also move forward using two credit spreads. In this case, the call spread would be above the current market price, and the put would be below the current market price.

You are only going to want to attempt the iron condor when trading in index options because they offer a unique mix of increased volatility coupled with a lower increase in risk. Additionally, it is important to put an iron condor into play only when you are extremely confident you know where the market is going. This is because the potential for loss, should you choose poorly, is very great. Assuming all goes according to plan you then stand to make a significant profit assuming the market doesn't move strongly in one direction or the other.

Iron Butterfly: To start an iron butterfly you want to use either a long or a short straddle and concurrently either purchase or sell a strangle based on the straddle you chose. While similar to a basic butterfly, this strategy utilizes both calls and puts rather than just one or the other. When done properly it limits the potential for profit or loss to the range of the strike prices that you set. This strategy is best used with options that are out of the money as they allow you to minimize both risk and cost.

The pair of options that you use in the iron butterfly should be set at a mid-strike point to generate either a short or a long straddle depending on if you are buying or selling. The so-called wings of the butterfly are formed from the pair of options at the lower strike price and the higher strike price that are generated once the strangle is sold. This helps to offset the long or short position which creates the limits regarding your total profits or losses.

Chapter 6: Advanced
Strategies to Try

Double diagonal strategy: In order to properly use the double diagonal strategy, you will start with a diagonal put spread along with a diagonal call spread. You can turn a horizontal spread into a diagonal spread by simply shifting the long leg to a new strike point with a different timeframe. Any spread where the two legs don't use the same month is said to be diagonal.

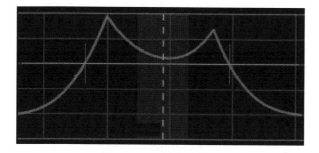

When using a diagonal call spread, you will need to combine a short call spread and a long calendar spread to allow it to move based on the rate at which time decay affects the option in question. Once you sell off the second call at the initial strike point, you will have backed into a spread for the short call. This will allow you to create a net credit which means that after the second call has been sold anything else you make is pure profit. A diagonal put works in largely the same way with the specifics reversed.

To run a double diagonal, you will start by putting a diagonal put spread and a diagonal call spread into play. This will provide you with the opportunity to profit from the increased time decay that front-month options experience when compared with back-month options.

To do so, you start with buying a put that is currently out of the money at a strike price that will be good for two months. At the same time, you will want to sell an out of the money put at a strike price that is good for one month. Furthermore, you are going to want to sell a call that is out of the money at a strike price that is good for one month. Finally, you will purchase a call at a separate strike price that is good for two months.

If everything goes according to plan, then the underlying asset will remain at a price that is between the second put and the first call. If the price remains above that pair of strike prices, then you are going to want to sell the options that are one month out. At the same time, you are going to want to sell another call with the same strike price as the call that is two months out.

When graphing this strategy, it is important to keep in mind that the profit and loss lines are not going to be as straight as you might expect because the two month options are still growing concerns. Straight lines and hard angles can only exist if the options you are graphing are all going to expire in the same timeframe.

While this strategy might seem extremely complicated at first, it can be made to seem much more manageable if you instead consider it as a form of profiting from a neutral amount of movement in the market, simply spread out into multiple expiration cycles.

The most useful time to use this strategy is when an underlying asset is halfway between the second put and the first call, the closer to the true midpoint the better. If the underlying asset isn't at this point, then biases towards bullishness or bearishness can skew the results. If the underlying asset remains at the midpoint, then the options you sold will expire without generating a profit, allowing you to keep a greater percentage of the premium.

This occurs because the first put and the second call that you purchased will help to decrease your overall risk, even if the underlying asset moves more than you might like. The goal of this strategy is to leave you with a net credit, though this is not always how things shake out. It is not a sure thing because the front month trades inherently have less time value which means that a net debit is a possibility. If this occurs, then you can make up the difference by selling the remaining options after the front month pair expires.

When the front month pair is close to expiring, and the price of the underlying asset is somewhere between the price of the second put and the first call then you are going to way to buy close to the pair of puts and create an additional put for sale at the second strike price along with a third call at the third strike price. These new options should have the same expiration as the other two month options. This is what is known as rolling out, and it can easily double, or even triple, your profits.

Leveraged covered call strategy: Also known as the fig leaf strategy, the leveraged covered call strategy is a great way to mitigate some of the risks that come along with trading options based on Long Term Equity Anticipation Securities (LEAPS). A standard LEAPS call is not set to expire for at least a year which means a short-term call lasts about 45 days. This strategy is useful if you feel somewhat bullish about the market's chances over this timeframe.

To utilize this strategy, you are going to start by purchasing a LEAPS call with access to a profitable strike price for the related underlying asset. At the same time, you are going to sell a call at a favorable strike price to ensure you can make a profit if you end up being assigned early. The goal here is to provide a covered call for the LEAPS transaction. While the two options you have committed two are similar, the fact that they have different expiration dates allows you to maximize your profits when compared with a standard covered call. Next, you are going to sell a call that is out of the money in the short term at the same strike price as the call. Ideally, the underlying asset will then stick close to the second strike price and not the first.

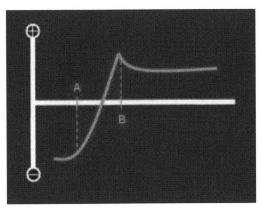

This strategy is useful if you don't want to put up all of the required capital right at the start. This, in turn, means that the premium that is generated as you sell the call is going to represent a larger percentage of your initial investment, leverage will ensure your profits are proportionally higher as well.

When graphing this strategy, be aware that your loss and profit lines will not be straight as the LEAPS call is going to remain open while the other call expires. You should also keep in mind that determining what your likely profits are going to be is tricky, in this instance, because the available data won't be reliable until enough time has passed to see where the LEAPs call is likely to end up.

When using the fig leaf strategy, your goal should be to purchase a LEAPS call that is going to move in the same way as the underlying asset. As such, it is recommended that you only consider calls that have a delta of .8 or higher. This means you are going to want to look at options that are at least 20 percent of the money. If you are considering an underlying asset that experiences a high degree of volatility, then options that are at least 40 percent of the money are recommended.

While this strategy is more useful in many situations than a traditional covered call, it is not with additional risks. First, unlike most underlying assets, LEAPS eventually expire which is something you need to take into account if you are to keep your investment. Second, being assigned on the short call can be cumbersome as you likely won't own the underlying asset when it occurs. You won't want to exercise your option to buy on the LEAPS call because you lose out on a significant amount of time value. The best solution is simply to hope that the short call expires out of the money and that you can sell it multiple times before the LEAPS call ultimately expires. Alternatively, you can sell the LEAPS call on the open market to ensure that you profit from the time value that remains. If you go this route, you are going to want to ensure that you also purchase the underlying asset to cover any short positions that might materialize.

This is an effective strategy if you have a clear idea of how an underlying asset is going to move but cannot currently afford to purchase it directly. If the price of this assets jumps the first strike price and heads right toward the second, then you can make an early profit by closing out the whole option.

Skip strike butterfly call spread: The biggest difference between a skip strike butterfly call spread and a traditional butterfly spread is that is much more directionally focused. With the skip strike version, you are going to want the underlying stock price to increase, though not beyond the limit of your secondary strike price. The calls at the second and fourth strike points will be nearly o though you will still retain the premium generated by the call at the primary strike price.

This strategy works by placing a short call spread into a butterfly long call spread. Essentially what you are doing is unloading the short call spread as a means of paying for the butterfly. While this would technically mean that you need to buy and sell a call at the same strike price, the results of this transaction would balance out so it can be skipped.

The spread on the short call allows for this strategy to be arranged with little extra cost in exchange for the chance at a significant gain. This also adds risk to the proceedings making the skip strike butterfly call spread riskier than a traditional butterfly spread. In order to get the best results from this strategy, you are going to want to ensure that all of the strike prices that you use are equidistance from one another while also expiring in the same month. The price of the underlying asset in question should then remain at or below the first strike price for the best results.

To use the skip strike butterfly call spread the first thing you are going to want to do is to purchase a call at the primary strike point. You will then want to sell a pair of calls at the second strike price. Finally, you are going to want to ignore the third strike price and purchase a call at the fourth strike price.

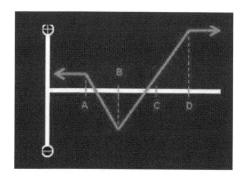

This is a terrific strategy to use if you are primarily interested in minimizing risk. This is the case because the underlying asset would need to see significant movement before breaking past the strike point for you to see serious losses. The risk with this strategy can be further mitigated if you utilize it with options based on indices instead of stocks because many indices experience very low volatility as conflicting internal price movements often cancel one another out.

This strategy is especially effective if you are bullish about the state of the market as it currently stands and where it is likely to go in the time frame that you have established. As long as you hit the third strike price, you can expect to make a profit even if the options are going to expire at a point that would traditionally allow you to break even. In order to make the maximum amount of profit, you would want to exercise the moment the underlying asset reaches the second strike price. You will then make a profit based on the second strike price subtracted by the first and any related fees.

Skip strike butterfly put spread: Much like the skip strike butterfly call spread, the put version skews more towards a directional strategy than the butterfly spread version. The biggest difference between the two is that while the traditional version hopes for the underlying asset to increase, the skip strike version hopes for the underlying asset to decrease in value, though not beyond the third strike price you have established.

As such, this is a good strategy to use if you are a little bearish on the state of the market as you will not want the underlying asset to decrease too far. If things work out as they should, you would then make no profit off of the first and second put, but you will earn a premium on the fourth put. This strategy works by establishing a short put spread inside a butterfly put spread that has a longer timeframe. Much like with the call variant, you can avoid buying and selling at the second strike point as these actions will cancel one another out. Furthermore, the short spread will provide you with the opportunity to use this strategy as a way to generate either a small debit or a positive credit. Like its counterpart, the skip strike butterfly put is riskier than the standard butterfly variation, though the potential for return is greater as well.

To start using this strategy, you will first purchase a put at the primary strike price. The second strike point can then be skipped as the two purchases cancel one another out. Next, you will purchase two puts at the third strike price. Finally, you will purchase a put at the fourth strike price. All the strike prices need to be equidistance from one another and have the same expiration month. For the best results, you will want the underlying asset price to remain at or above the third strike price.

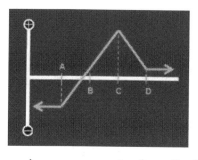

In order to make as much as possible from this strategy, you are going to want to execute the moment the underlying asset reaches the third strike price. The maximum amount of profit from this strategy is limited to the difference between the final two strike prices, minus any additional fees. In order to break even with this strategy, and still generate a credit, you will need the underlying asset to remain at or above the secondary strike price. On the other hand, if the trade was set up to generate a net debit then you will be able to break even at the fourth strike price as well as the second.

CONCLUSION

Thank for making it through to the end of *Options Trading: The Ultimate Guide to Options Trading*, let's hope it was informative and able to provide you with all of the tools you need to achieve your financial goals, whatever it is that they may be. Just because you've finished this book doesn't mean there is nothing left to learn on the topic, expanding your horizons is the only way to find the mastery you seek.

The next step is to stop reading already and to get ready to start trading options as effectively as possible. With the strategies and tips provided in the preceding chapters, you should have the tools you need to be successful regardless of the current state of the market. This isn't a sure thing, however, and only by taking the time to truly analyze not only the current state of the market but also the current and likely future state of the options you are interested in can you maximize your trade percentage as completely as possible. While it can be difficult to know the right move early on in your trading career, if you trust yourself throughout, then eventually that trust will be justified.

Just because you are now armed with everything you need to trade options successfully, doesn't mean that you can expect the profits to start rolling in right away. It is important to keep the right mindset, day in and day out if you hope to be a successful options trader in the long term. No matter how good you are, major windfalls are rare and chasing them is only going to cause your trading capital to dwindle. It is always going to be a better choice to take solid, reliable profits over riskier alternatives; remember options trading is a marathon, not a sprint, slow and steady wins the race.

A BEGINNER'S GUIDE TO DAY TRADING: DISCOVER HOW TO BE A DAY TRADING KING

DESCRIPTION

Day trading is often a misunderstood investment, but it can be one of the best if you want to make money now, rather than waiting for the long term. You will work in the stock market, but instead of making a purchase and holding onto a stock for months and even years, the day trader will make purchases and sales of the same stock, all in one day. It is an exciting investment opportunity, but it is important to learn some strategies to get the most out of your investment.

Inside this guidebook, we are going to learn the steps for success in day trading. Some of the topics we will explore include:

- The basics of day trading
- The rules for success
- How to complete a key analysis to master day trading
- Further analysis on how to succeed at day trading
- Additional day trading strategies
- The best platforms for day traders

When you are ready to put your money to work with a great investment opportunity that provides you with an income each day, day trading is the answer for you. Check out this guidebook and learn everything that you need to know to get started in day trading.

INTRODUCTION

Congratulations on downloading your personal copy of *A Beginner's Guide to Day Trading: Discover How to Be a Day Trading King.* Thank you for doing so.

The following chapters will discuss some of the many things that you should know to get started with day trading. Day trading can be a great way to make money from purchasing and selling your stocks all in one day. We will discuss some of the basics of day trading, as well as many of the different strategies that you can use, such as a fundamental analysis and a technical analysis, to make sure that you see success in this investment.

There are many different options with day trading and if you work on your research ahead of time, it is easy to make a good income. Day trading has gotten a bad name because many beginners turn it into a gamble, taking on more risks than necessary and losing out on everything. But a true day trader will do the research, weigh the risks, and make decisions that limit their losses.

When you are ready to learn the different aspects of day trading and how to make this investment work, check out this guidebook and learn all about day trading for your needs.

There are plenty of books on this subject on the market, thanks again for choosing this one! Every effort was made to ensure it is full of as much useful information as possible. Please enjoy!

CHAPTER 1: THE BASICS OF DAY TRADING

Investing your money is a smart financial move to help your income grow without having to put in more hours in the office each day. There are quite a few investment options that you can choose to go with depending on your interests, amount of time available, and how much money you would like to earn. Some investors like the idea of placing their money into a retirement plan and keeping it safe there. Some investors like being in the real estate market and owning property to make their money. Investing comes in many shapes and forms and the trick is finding the option that works for you.

But an option that many investors miss out on because they simply don't know about it is working on day trading. This is a form of investing in the stock market, but rather than holding onto a stock for a few years or longer, you will make your purchases as well as your sales all in the same day. This requires a good understanding of the stock market, the trends that are going on in the economy, and understand how quickly the market can turn in just a day.

With your day trading, you will need to pick out the stocks you want to purchase, make the purchase, and then sell them by the end of the day to make a profit. There are a few different strategies that go with this and often they make just small profits per each one, but when you add these together over a few days, you are going to see some results of huge profits for you. Some traders choose to borrow money in order to take advantage of some of the smaller price movements in the market, but you should be careful with this in the beginning.

Before you make a purchase, you need to understand the market well enough to know that there will be an increase in the value of the stock during that day. While most stocks stay fairly steady over the years, slowly going up a little bit over the long term, there are quite a few fluctuations that can occur in that stock from day to day. This is where the day trader will be able to make their money. They can take the variations that occur in a stock during the day and predict where it will go before making the purchase and hopefully seeing a profit.

The main idea with day trading is that you will be able to enter the market at the beginning of the day, looking for a stock that has a low price. After a bit of research on this stock, which you have probably been doing for a bit beforehand anyway, you will expect that the price of that stock will go up by the end of the day at the latest. With the right plan in place ahead of time, you will purchase that stock at the low price and then by the end of the day sell it for a higher price to make your profit.

There are many factors that come into play concerning the amount of profit that you will make. The amount that you paid for the stock, how high the stock goes during that day, and whether you released the stock before prices started falling again will all determine how much you are able to make. When it comes to day trading, you often will not make a big profit on individual stocks because of the brevity of your trading. But when you make many trades throughout the day and do this each day, you can start to make a good income with day trading.

As a beginner, it is important to realize that day trading can be a great way to make a profit in the stock market relatively quickly, but it is also possible to lose some money in the stock market as well. This is a risky investment because the time period is so short in day trading and often this results in inconsistencies and issues with watching the trends. Over time, you will become more familiar with the charts and tables for the stock market and you will be able to make better predictions.

The next question that many beginners have is what they are able to purchase and sell in day trading. The good news, you will be able to trade in anything that you want on the stock market. Many people stick with equity stocks because of all the options that come with them, but you could branch out to other components if you wish for day trading. Even penny stocks can be useful, but most beginners stay away from this because there aren't that many buyers and sellers, which makes it hard to do the trading in one day.

One niche that is popular with day trading is currencies through Forex. This specialty will need some research and knowledge of the market, but it can work well since there is a high volatility and liquidity for these options. If you do trade in currencies, make sure that you keep updated on the various currency exchanges; just a little shift in one could cause shifts in other currencies as well.

These are a few of the niches that are popular with more experienced day traders, but as a beginner, it is best to stick with the stock market. The stock market poses the lowest risk and you will be able to pull up a lot of charts and details to help you make accurate predictions. The liquidity is also there so you shouldn't have issues with purchasing and selling the stocks that you want to trade that way and since the stock market is full of options that stay on a consistent pattern, you can really start to see which ones will work for you.

The benefits of day trading

Day trading is a great investment option that you can choose when first starting out. Whether you decide to do this on the side to learn the ropes and make your money grow, or you are looking to turn this into a full-time income, there are options for everyone who would like to get started.

The first benefit of day trading is that you will not have to worry about overnight risks. Many other stock market investments have issues with what can happen to the stock overnight. This can be especially true if you work on stocks in other countries, or ones that rely on these other countries, because a lot can change in that time. When you choose day trading, you will be able to make all of your purchases and all of the sales in one day, finishing up before you go to bed that night. As a day trader, you are not going to be concerned about what happens to the market that night. Worst case scenario, you just take a day off from trading if the market goes way south and you don't see it going back up.

Many traders like day trading because it provides them with a lot of options. You are able to pick from working on the stock market to picking options, to work on securities, and even working with different currencies if you would like. As the trader, you need to decide which market you are most comfortable working in before starting.

The options for the strategies you are able to use provide a lot of variety in day trading. Each trader has their own strategy in this game and many times more than one strategy is going to work to bring you money. It is your responsibility to learn more about the strategies, which we will discuss in more detail later, and then stick with the one you choose. As you get more familiar with a strategy, t will become easier to recognize the stocks and options that fit with it, and you will see your income grow.

If you are a trader who likes to research your options and likes to make sound decisions based on this research, day trading will be the right option for you. This means that to see success, you need to make sure you think logically about your choices, rather than letting your emotions get in the way. For those who let their emotions get in the way of their decisions, it is best to pick another option because day trading is not going to work well for you. But if you are willing to research a plan and stick with that no matter what the market does, you will come out on top.

As a day trader, you are going to appreciate the high profits you can earn in a short amount of time. Once you get into your rhythm and learn how to work with day trading, you will find that this investment can make you a lot of money in a relatively short amount of time. If you are successful, you can make your profits in just one day, much faster than you are able to do with pretty much any other investment.

What some people don't understand about day trading, which s why many of them don't get into this market, is that you actually have some control over the amount of risk that you are taking. This trading option does have some risks, but if you pick out a good strategy, learn how to keep the emotions out of it, and make sound decisions, you will find that you control a lot of your risks with this investment.

Being ready for quick decisions

In order to see success with day trading, you need to be able to work fast inside of the market. You will be making your purchases and your sales of the stock within one day. You don't get the benefit of holding onto the stocks and riding out the market for the long term like in other investments, so your decisions need to be quick. You have to recognize the daily trends and when a stock will go up and down within just a few hours, and this can be risky and tough for some people to work with.

If you are someone who likes to hold onto stocks for some time, or you aren't good at making decisions quickly, the day trading investment is not the right one for you. While you can take some time to look over the different stocks and get used to the graphs and the different aspects of your chosen stocks, you will need to be able to make the purchase and know when to let it go all in the same day. For some people, this can be too stressful to handle and they will want to pick out an option that gives them longer term results.

Personality traits for day trading

Before you decide to look at day trading, you need to make sure that you have the right personality type. There are some people who will do amazing at day trading because they are able to do research, avoid the emotions, and just make sound decisions. On the other hand, there are some people who are too emotional, can't make quick decisions, and are just not that great at working in this kind of investment. Some of the personality traits that are needed to see success in day trading include:

- Not ruled by your emotions: as a day trader, you must make sure that you are not allowing your decisions to be controlled by your emotions. If you allow the emotions to come into play, you can end up holding onto stocks that are losing you money, picking out the wrong stocks, and just doing poorly overall on your investment. You must be someone who is levelheaded before being able to work on day trading and actually see success.

- Willing to take some risks: day trading is pretty risky to get into. You are able to reduce some of the risks that you are taking, but since you are required to purchase and sell the stocks all in one day, the risk factor is going to be higher compared to some of the longer-term investments that you can work within the stock market. While long-term investments allow you to ride the ups and downs of the market, but day trading is over such a short time that you will have to be really good at guessing the trends because if they go down, it is unlikely to be enough time to go back up.

- Good at recognizing trends in the market: if you look at the charts for a particular company and you are not able to see some of the trends over time, this is not the right option for you to get into. Unless there are some big changes in the company, most stocks will have some trends that you can use to help make your decisions.

- Willing to research and read the news: It is impossible to be successful if you just pick a stock and hope it works out. Successful day traders are able to get started in this market because they research what they are doing. They are very familiar with the trends for their stock and know exactly when to make the purchases and when to sell them. They also take some time each day to read through the local, national, and even international news to see if any changes will occur in the market that could affect their stocks.

Day trading is not an investment that works for everyone. Some people will find a lot of success with this investment, and others will not be able to make it work. But if you have some of the personality traits from above, and you are sure to find that day trading is the perfect investment option for you.

Understanding your goals for day trading

Before we get into the day trading game, it is important to understand some of your goals. There are many different reasons that investors choose to go with day trading, but your reason is going to help you to make your decisions. Keep in mind that there is a level of risk that comes with day trading and depending on where you are in life, and what you would like to accomplish with day trading, you may make different decisions.

For example, if you are in your 20s and just starting out, you may be willing to take more risks. You have time left to work on your retirement or to try some of the other investment options if day trading doesn't work out for you so you will take some of the bigger risks. But, if you are in your late 50s, you may want to work on putting money on your retirement rather than losing it all so close to this time, and so the risks that you take with day trading may be lower.

Understanding where you are in life and what you would like to do with your investment will help you to decide what stocks to purchase, how much you would like to make from this investment, and much more. Either way, you still need to work on doing your research and learning about the market ahead of time to ensure you get the best results inside this investment.

Understanding how you react to different situations is also going to be important when you work on day trading. Some people are more inclined to doing well with day trading because they are able to research the options, think through their decisions, and will stick with their plans no matter what. They understand when the market is going down and won't go back up, and they know when it is time to pull out of the game, even if they are losing money. They can cut their losses, making it easier to do well later on, rather than holding onto a dying stock and losing even more money.

If you are able to stay with this kind of mindset while trading, day trading can be a great option for you to choose. But, if you are someone who is controlled by their emotions, someone who will hold onto a stock as it rises, just to see it lose money rather than stick with the plan, or someone who holds out hope that the stock will go back up rather than cutting your losses, day trading is not something that you should consider.

Day trading can be a great way to earn some money while investing in the stock market. Instead of waiting for years to get your income like traditional investing, day trading allows you a way to earn money each day. You will need to spend some time researching and coming up with a good strategy to pick the right stocks, but with some practice, you will make a good profit on your day trading endeavors.

CHAPTER 2: WHAT ARE THE
RULES OF SUCCESS?

Now that we know a bit more about day trading, it is time to learn a few rules that will lead us to success. This is an exciting time, but learning the right steps to ensure success can help even the beginner to do a great job. You will find that day trading can be completely different compared to some of the other investments that you choose because all the work happens within a single day. You won't have a lot of time to ride the ups and downs of the system, so understanding the market ahead of time can make a big difference.

If you have decided that day trading is the option for you to make money from an investment, there are a couple rules that beginners can follow in order to help them to avoid mistakes and do well with this option. Some of the rules that day traders can use to actually earn money from the beginning, rather than hoping it will all work well and losing out, includes:

Understand the three E's:

The three E's of day trading include enter, exit, and escape. Before you even enter the market, you need to have a plan prepared. This plan needs to include an enter price, a price that the stock should be at before you are willing to make a purchase. Then it needs to have an exit price, or the price that the stock will reach and you will sell, no matter what happens during the rest of the day. Having an exit strategy can be helpful as well in case the price starts to drop so that you can limit your losses.

Having this plan in place will help you to make as much as possible, without missing out when the market goes back down. When you set these points, make sure that you stick with these. As a beginner, you may let your emotions get in the way of smart decisions, but if you set up this plan and stick with it, it is much easier to make money with day trading.

Wait to trade

When making your trades, you should wait to make purchases until after the market opens. There are a lot of changes that occur during the first fifteen to twenty minutes in the stock market and it is hard to predict how the market will play out. Wait for a few minutes at least and then make your purchase when things level out a little bit. Once you see that the craziness of the first few minutes fades out, you can make a purchase knowing that the trends you have studied will be in play.

It is tempting to get into the market right when it opens, but there is a lot of fluctuation that occurs here and a position that looked good at opening can quickly change. It is only fifteen minutes to wait, so why not just enjoy that cup of coffee a bit longer and then go in and do your trading after that time occurs.

Avoid the margin

As a beginner, you may be tempted to use the margin to help increase your profits in day trading. When you are using the margin, it is basically like taking out a loan from the brokerage firm. You can take out this money to pay for part of the investment or all of it, but this can lead to some big problems for the beginner. Some experts will use the margin to help them increase their potential returns, but for beginners, it is best to never spend more money than you can afford to lose. If you end up using the margin and the trade goes against you, you are going to end up losing twice as much. It is a huge risk for a beginner who is not used to the market and until you perfect your strategy if ever, you shouldn't use the margin.

When you first get started with day trading, you should stick with just using your own money to make the trades. It can be dangerous to borrow money from the brokerage firm, they are mostly offering it in the hopes of making extra money, and just use the money that you have available and are willing to lose.

The best thing you can do for day trading is to only spend money that you have readily available. This may mean that you have to start small with just a few trades or you will need to save up for a bit in order to reach this point, but it is always for the best. Betting more money than you have can make day trading into a gamble and using the margin means that you could lose out on twice as much money when it is all said and done. Protect your investment and only use the money that you are able to use.

Set up your plan for selling

Most investors are going to just think about entering in the stock market, but they forget to come up with a strategy for selling their stocks. But if you want to make a profit, you have to sell the stock at some point. Without a good strategy, you will find that you will miss out on some of the profits you could make, and you may even hold onto the stock too long and lose a lot of money in the process.

When you enter the market, determine when you would like to get out of the market. How much profit is good for you before you exit the market? It is not a good idea to ride out the market because while some people are lucky and can get out at a higher profit, many times the market turns suddenly, and you may lose out or make a lower profit. Decide what exit point you would like to meet, and then sell when you reach that point, regardless of whether the stock continues to go up or not.

Take notes along the way

As a beginner, things are going to be pretty new to you and you may need to try out a few different options before finding the path that helps you. But if you are trying out different things, working in different markets, and more, it is easy to forget what works and what doesn't over time. It is a good idea to write down some of your strategies over time so you can look back at them when needed. You will honestly learn more from your mistakes than from your successes, but this is how you grow your profit in day trading.

When you first start with day trading, make sure to purchase a small journal and then take a few notes about all of the trades that you work on. Even if t was a small trade, a trade that went really well, one that went poorly, or one that didn't really do much, it is important to write down the details. You never know when a new trade comes up and you can use the notes that you wrote down earlier to help you become successful.

Try practicing

Practicing how day trading works is a good way to gain confidence in the investment and to try out a few different strategies It can also help you to see f you are really cut out to do day trading or if you should try out a different method of investing before you lose out on a lot of money. Many brokerage firms have trial accounts that let you input your own numbers to experiment with so you can try it out.

Whether you think you need it or not, try out the trial account. Choose realistic numbers to start out with so you can see how much you would really earn or lose in day trading. For example, if you plan to put in $10,000 to start, it doesn't make much sense to experiment with $100,000 in the trial account. Take this part seriously so you can see how you would actually do when playing with real money.

Pick out reputable sources

When it comes to day trading, you want to make sure you are picking out sources that give you accurate and timely information. You have a lot riding on this information and it would be a shame to pick out the wrong stocks or sell at the wrong time because your sources were not all that great. It is important to look for how your sources will benefit from your actions. Some sources simply want you to make a purchase because it helps them make a profit, but then will dump you as soon as they sell to you. Learn how to follow some of your own judgment and you will make the right choices.

Be prepared to cut your losses

Most beginners are excited to get into the stock market and start earning money from day trading. And with some good research and picking out a good strategy, you can make profits from this option. But you also need to be ready to lose money as well. There are times when the stock that you choose isn't going to do so well, and learning how to cut your losses can make the difference between losing a little bit of money, and losing a lot of money. Some beginners are so desperate to make money in day trading that they will continue to hold onto the stock while the price keeps plummeting.

Before you purchase a stock, decide when you will exit the game. Once the stock reaches that low point, you sell, regardless of it being a loss or the potential for it to go back up later on. Yes, there is the possibility of the stock going up, but you can always repurchase and try again. But if you held on to that stock hoping the market would go back up, you could end up losing a lot of money in the process.

Learning how the day trading market works does take some time and effort. Beginners need to have a good understanding of how the market works and you should be able to pick out the right strategy that will help you to make the most profit. No matter where you are in your journey of day trading investing, make sure to follow some of these simple rules and you will see success.

Common mistakes to avoid

In addition to following some of the rules listed above, it is important to understand the common mistakes most beginners run into when they start day trading. Some of these mistakes are pretty obvious, but when you are in the trade and trying to make a profit, you may find that it is easier to make these mistakes than not. Some of the most common mistakes to avoid in day trading include:

- Lack of preparation: day trading is not a form of gambling unless you aren't prepared. You can't win in this investment simply with luck on your side. When you win, it is because you took the time to plan out your strategy and to think out your moves. Beginners need to educate themselves about day trading, look through the information that is available to them, and learn how to make informed decisions if they want to make a profit.

- Not using all the tools available: day trading does require some tools to help the trader be successful. You should consider adding many of them to your strategy to get the best results. Some of the tools that you can include are educational resources, charts and graphs, trading software, and brokers. Without some of these tools to help you out, you will find that it is hard to trade.

- Keep it small: many beginners are tempted to go big when they get into this investment. They want to make a lot of money right away. But this is not the proper way to be successful in day trading over the long term. This kind of go big attitude turns our investment into more of a gamble, which also makes it more likely that you will lose money as well. It is just fine to look for smaller profits in day trading because this helps to reduce your risks.

- Averaging down: this is a mistake that could take a small loss, and turn it into a big one that will ruin your whole account. Sometimes t is tempting to think that since a stock is considered cheap at $5, it is an even better deal when it reaches $4. But using this method means that you are basically choosing a stock that is at a losing position. It is best to not pick this stock in the first place because it is likely to go to a lower price soon, and if you already own the stock, it is time to cut your losses.

- Holding onto the stock too long: it can be hard to lose in day trading, but holding onto a stock for too long results in really big losses. If you have a plan for cutting your losses, you may still lose a little bit of money, but it helps you to look at the market logically and not hold onto a stock so long that you lose your whole portfolio.

- Avoid vengeance trading: this is a common mistake that many investors get into and it can cause you to have to leave day trading pretty quickly. With this one, you may have just lost out on $600 on one particular trade, but you will go and search for a trade that is of equal value in order to make that money back. It is always a good idea to look for new trades that will help you earn a profit, but if you are just choosing stocks because they could potentially bring that loss back to you, you will end up losing more in the long run.

Day trading is hard enough on its own. You have to balance a lot of plates and make decisions quickly in order to make the purchases and the sales all in one day. Make sure to avoid some of the common mistakes listed above to ensure you are not inadvertently costing yourself a lot of money in trades.

CHAPTER 3: A KEY ANALYSIS ON HOW TO MASTER DAY TRADING

So now that we know a bit about the basics of day trading, it is time to learn some of the strategies that you can use to help make your trades profitable. A technical analysis is one of the best strategies to use in day trading because it allows you to take many different aspects of the stock into consideration before making the purchase. Unlike some of the other strategies, the technical analysis is not going to have you look at the stock or all the fundamentals because you are really just holding onto this stock for a day or less, so these don't matter as much.

The short-term trades in day trading is what makes this a different type of investment compared to some others in the stock market. You aren't going to worry so much about how solid the company is because you are just worried about how it will behave today. If the stock ends up going downhill after today, you can always look for another option. In day trading, there are a few things that you will need to understand and watch out for to help you to pick out the right stocks including:

- Volatility: to see success, you need to see that the market is moving and that the price of your stocks is not stuck in one place. If you look at the price of the stock and see that it doesn't have fluctuations in the price, it is not a good one to invest in. Preferably, you will want to find a stock that starts out at a low price point but will go up during the day so you can increase your profits. When looking at the charts for a particular stock, you want to see it go up and down in some sort of pattern; this pattern will help you to determine when you should enter and when you should sell the stock.

- Liquidity: not only are you looking for the price of the stock to move throughout the day, you need to make sure that there is enough trading volume of the stock for it to be worth your time. Nothing is worse than getting a stock and making the investment, just to find out that no one else is interested in the stock and you are stuck with it. Look for a stock that not only has a pattern with the price point but will also provide you with enough buyers and sellers so you can leave the market when you want.

The parts of a technical analysis

To start a technical analysis, there are a few factors that will come into play to help you see success. Learning these parts and understanding how they work will help you to pick the right stocks and earn a profit as well. The main parts of a technical analysis include:

Volatility

So the first thing we want to look for when working on a technical analysis is the volatility of the stock. You will notice when looking at the stock market that there are plenty of shares that are traded in the various markets, and these trading decisions are going to be made by investors and traders, all of which are going to try and keep their own interests in the forefront without really caring about how others do in the market.

If the prices of the stocks are moving around, this means that there are many investors who are purchasing and selling the stock. This is good news for the day trader because you have a better chance of finding options that can be profitable for you. You may notice that when big events go on with a company, the volatility of that stock will change as well and this can help you to earn more if you can make the purchase before prices go up; this is why watching the news and trends in the market can be very beneficial to you.

As a beginner, it is important to learn how to recognize the signs of volatility inside the market and see the patterns that happen. This will help you to understand when there is a lot of movement in a particular stock and can make it so you get in when the prices are low and sell when they are high.

Liquidity

When you hear the word liquidity inside the stock market, you most likely hear it when people talk about how much trading is going on with your stock. Since day traders are working on a limited amount of time to make their purchases and their sales, they don't want to end up in a situation where they aren't able to find someone to purchase their stocks later on. A market that is liquid is considered good because it provides the investor with opportunities to make some good purchases while also allowing them to find a buyer later on whether the market goes up or down.

As you get into this investment, you will start to notice that there are some markets that aren't liquid. In these markets, you will find that it is hard to purchase stocks and it is almost impossible to sell them later on, especially when you only have a few hours to do both. Without the opportunity to make purchases and sales, it is hard to make a profit in day trading so it is important to stay out of these markets altogether.

Pivot points, resistance, and support

All of these are points that you should know about to make a technical analysis. They are all mathematical equations that can take the recent performance of your chosen stock and will help you to see if they are good to work with. The first one is the pivot point and to work with this one, you will need to get information from the closing from the day before; specifically, you need to find the high, low, and the close from the previous day. Then you are able to use this formula to come up with the pivot point:

(high + low + close)/3

Remember that you are able to get this information from the previous day. Using the pivot point can be a great way to start because they reflect the different trading levels that are the most recent and when you take a look at them, you will be able to notice whether some shifts are on the way. Or example, if you notice that the stock is going higher than your pivot point, your closing is most likely going to end up higher than the previous day, as long as something drastic doesn't happen during the day. If you notice that the stock prices are lower than the pivot point, the closing will end up lower than the previous day.

Now that we understand a bit about the pivot points, you are able to use this information in order to figure out the resistance levels and the support levels. The formulas that you need to find out these points include:

$S_1 = (P * 2) - High$

$S_2 = (P * 2) - (High - Low)$

$R_1 = (P * 2) - Low$

$R_2 = P - (High - Low)$

The resistance level is basically the price that the stock will not go above for at least that day because it is too high. If a stock does go above the resistance level, this is called a breakout and usually, there was a big event that caused this to happen that the numbers would not show at all. The support level is the level that the stock will not go below, and it follows the same idea as the resistance level. In most cases, as long as external events stay the same, the stock is going to remain pretty consistent.

When trying to figure out the resistance level, you will not only need to use the formulas above, you will also need to bring out some of the charts and graphs and look at the history of your chosen stock over the past few months. For example, if you are looking at these charts and you notice that the stock never seems to go above $30, but it gets close, over that time period, this is probably your resistance level. For some reason, investors are willing to hold onto the stock until it reaches about $30, but then they sell it off. Unless some dramatic changes occur, the stock will not get above this amount, and this would be the place where you would want to sell the stock to make your profit.

This is just a part of your strategy, though. You now know where you would like to sell the stock based on the history of the stock and its resistance level, but when should you purchase the stock to get the biggest return on investment. This is where the support level will come into play.

When working on the support level, you ae looking at the point on the graph that shows how low the stock will go. When looking at the formulas that are above and the charts for the stock, you will notice that over a few months, the stock doesn't seem to go below a certain level. For some reason, other investors feel that when the stock reaches the support level, it has become a good value and they will start purchasing again. You would want to purchase the stock as close to the support level as possible to help you to make the biggest profit.

This helps you to come up with the strategy that you want to use. You will want to purchase the stock when it gets close to the support level so you can get the best deal on this stock. Then when you notice the stock is getting close to the resistance level, you will want to sell the stock before the price goes back down. Say that the support level is $10 for the stock and the resistance is $30; you would want to try to purchase the stocks for the $10 and sell them for as close to the $30 as possible, making a $20 profit on each stock in the process.

Many people like to use the technical analysis to help them make decisions on which stocks to purchase. You have some great formulas to work with and even the history of the stock to back up your decisions. You do need to keep track of the news and any shifts in the company as well because these can cause dramatic shifts in the stock that go away from the history that is in the charts, but for many stocks that remain steady, this is a great way to get started because the numbers stay pretty consistent and it is easier for beginners to get started with. It is not the only method to use, but it is pretty secure for making at least a little profit each day in day trading.

CHAPTER 4: FURTHER ANALYSIS ON HOW TO SUCCEED AT DAY TRADING

While the technical analysis is a good option for beginners to get started with, there are other options that you are able to use in order to help you to make smart decisions in day trading. The next one that we will talk about is the fundamental analysis because it will look at a few more aspects of the stock other than the up and down movements that occur on the charts. With the fundamental analysis, we are going to take a look at some of the specifics of the company rather than just what is on a chart. For example, the fundamental analysis would look at things like the revenue versus the debt, how strong the company is, brand recognition, and more about the company. It helps you to see if the company is in a good place in the market based on how the company is organized and run.

In this chapter, we are going to take a look at some of the aspects that are needed to perform a fundamental analysis. It is going to rely less on the charts and graphs that were used in the technical analysis, but t looks at some specific aspects of the company to ensure that it is being managed properly to see a return on investment.

Fundamental analysis

A fundamental analysis can be another method to help you pick the stocks that you want to trade with and even when to enter and exit the market. Some people choose to work with just a fundamental analysis and others will combine this with the technical analysis we discussed a bit earlier. When we use a fundamental analysis inside of the stock market, we are focusing on some of the underlying factors that can affect how the company runs and how it will react in the future. It is possible to use this type of analysis regardless of whether you are talking about the industry or the economy. It is often a term that can be used in order to refer to the wellbeing of the stock inside the economy, not just a look at the price movements of the stock.

There are a few questions that day traders should ask that concern the company you want to trade in when using the fundamental analysis. These questions include:

- Is the company seeing a growth in revenue?
- Is the company able to bring in some kind of profit and if they are, how much profit do they bring in.
- Can you tell if the company is in a position that is strong enough to beat out their competition, both now and in the future?
- Is there potentially any issues with the company being able to repay their debts?
- Is there any potential within with the management and are they behaving in an ethical manner?

These questions may seem simple, but they will actually require you to do some research on any company that you want to purchase stocks from. While there are a few questions that you asked above, it all boils down to one main question: is this a good company that is strong and has stock that you are able to trust?

A fundamental analysis is going to consider two different factors to help you make your decisions. First, we are going to look at the quantitative information or the information that you are able to measure out in numerical terms. Fundamental analysis will also require qualitative research, or the character or the quality of something, such as the quality of a company, rather than how big or small the company may be.

When working on your trades, you will find that quantitative information is most often used because it allows you to look at a lot of numbers. These numbers will give you insight into how the company is doing and if they are performing in a manner that can make you some money. For example, if you look at the financial statements of the business, you will be able to find the quantitative data about that company. But, if you are looking for some of the qualitative features of that same company, it is going to be a bit harder to find. This information would include things like the name recognition of the company and who runs the company, both of which can be harder to rate.

It is possible to find companies that have both high qualitative and quantitative features at the same time. For example, when we look at the Coca-Cola company, we will notice that it meets both of these categories. This company as a great financial sheet, where they are able to pay off their bills and still bring in a high revenue. In addition, this company also has a good reputation, one that people know about and trust. Even though this company does have a combination of both features, it is often not a good one to use for day trading because the stock is already close to its peak, without really reaching a low point, but it shows how both categories can come together.

It is possible to combine together the fundamental analysis with the technical analysis. There are some things that are missing from both of these analyses, but combining them together can help you to fill in the gaps and makes it easier to get the results that you want. For example, you wouldn't want to pick out a company just because it does well with the fundamental analysis. The company may be good, but if it has already reached its peak, it is unlikely that you can make money from this option. Of course, you could also miss out if you avoid a company that has been stagnant for a bit of time, but has good name recognition and will have some big news released soon that changes where the stocks go. Combining the two analysis together will help you to make the decisions that are needed to pick out good stocks for day trading.

The trick with working inside of day trading is to learn how to put both the technical analysis and the fundamental analysis together. When both of these tools work together, they can give you more confidence on the stocks that you pick and with some practice, you will be able to make a great income from day trading.

Gambling and Speculation

One area that some new traders get confused about when starting day trading is how it differs from speculation and gambling. For one, if you work on day trading the right way, you can actually make money. It is not about chance like gambling is, day trading is more about careful planning and research to pick out the best stocks that will earn you a profit.

One of the main differences that you can see between speculation and investing is the risks that are taken for the trade. With day trading, you get to choose the amount of risk that you would like to take and the amount you choose will directly correlate with the amount that you can make. Most beginners will start with a low-risk option to learn the game and then when they get more familiar with it, they can increase the risk. The more risks that you take on, the more your day trading can become like a gamble because the risk will become so high that you lose control.

In speculation, you will choose to trade on all of the high-risk options, sometimes they don't even spend time looking over charts or determining which process is the best one for them to go with. They will see that a stock has a high reward attached with it and will just choose to trade on that one. If you are correct, you will make a huge amount of profit, but since the risk is so high, you are more likely to loose out big when you speculate, which is why the high-risk options in day trading become like gambling.

Most day traders are not going to work in this way. They understand that they could make higher profits from some of the higher risk stocks, but they are also conscious of the fact that they could lose a lot of money as well. They are more comfortable with being in control of their investments so they will choose lower risk options that may yield a lower return but makes it more likely they will at least get something back from the trade.

No matter what strategy you pick for day trading, you must make sure that you are thinking like an investor, not a gambler. When you think about the stock market as a gambler, you are more likely to take risks that are not necessary, allow your emotions to get into the mix, and end up losing a lot of money in the process. But when you think about the stock market as an investment, you are more likely to think your decisions through and you will gather the information that is needed to actually make some money. The gamblers are the ones who give day trading a bad name because they do end up failing and losing a ton of money in the process. But when you act like an investor with day trading, you are sure to see your income grow.

Learning how to do the right kind of analysis, either the technical analysis or the fundamental analysis, you are going to learn how to understand the market and how it works, and you will be able to use this information in order to get the most out of all trades. As you learn how the market is going to work, you may make a few bad trades in the process (something that even professional investors see happen on occasion). But over time you will get pretty good at reading the market and you can make the right decisions, with the right amount of risk that you are comfortable with, in order to find success with day trading.

CHAPTER 5: ADDITIONAL DAY TRADING STRATEGIES

The technical analysis and the fundamental analysis are great places to start when it comes to working in day trading, but you also need to work on a good strategy to make sure you are picking the stocks that work the best for you. There are actually quite a few different strategies that will work in day trading, but it is important to understand how they work because all of them work a little bit differently. They can all be successful so you simply need to pick the one that works the best for you and then stick with it.

It is sometimes tempting to skip around from one strategy to another when you first start out because you are uncertain about how all of them work or you are uncertain about how each one will work. But you need to pick just one strategy, learn how to use it properly, and then stick with it so that you can see success. Here we are going to talk about some of the best day trading strategies that you can use and while they don't guarantee success every time when used properly, they can increase your chances of getting a good return on investment from your day trading endeavors.

News trading

One strategy that is pretty successful in day trading is called news trading. With this strategy, you are able to predict some big changes that will happen in the stock market, or for a particular stock, before others can catch on to the news. When this strategy is successful, you are able to purchase the stocks that you would like before the news is released, usually at a lower price. Then when the news breaks, you will be able to sell the stock at a higher price so you can make a good profit.

This strategy is going to require you to do quite a bit of research ahead of time. You need to be able to read the news and recognize some signs in different stocks to tell when a big change will occur to change the value. You will find that some of the news is going to help increase how much the stock is worth. You would want to purchase the stock before the news breaks so you can get it for a low price and then when the news comes out, you can sell the stock when the price goes up. On the other side of things, it is also possible to read the news and realize when a stock is about to go down in price. If you already own the stock, you would want to sell it quickly before you lose out or you would want to avoid purchasing this stock at all since the price is likely to go down.

Range trading

144

Another strategy that can help beginners make some money in day trading is known as range trading. With this strategy, you are able to identify the overbought and oversold areas for the stock. For this one, you need to be able to look at the support and the resistant areas. This is the one that you will want to work on if you notice that there are a few markets that end up meandering, or in markets that there seems to be a lot of up and down in the market, but you aren't able to find a trend or a pattern that goes with them.

Pairs trading

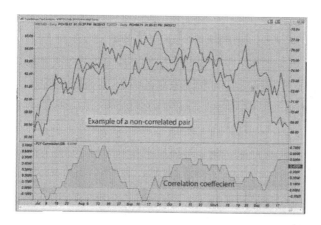

Many beginners like to work with the strategy that is called pairs trading. This strategy helps you to remain neutral in the market and it can match together a short position with a long position so you reduce your risks and can make some good money in the process. When you are a pairs trader, you are going to look for some weaknesses to occur in the market before going long on a stock that is underperforming and then going short on the stock that is over performing. This will effectively close up the position so when the gap closes back up, the market gets back to normal and you are able to make a profit from these positions.

You will find that the profit you are able to get from pairs strategy is going to come from the difference in price that will occur between your two instruments, or your two stocks, rather than from where they are both able to go inside the market. Basically what this means is that you will be able to get a profit if the long position goes up more than the short one, and you can make a profit can be made if the short position ends up going down more than the long one. This is why pairs trading can be so successful; it is possible to earn some money on different market conditions, even if there is an issue with low or high volatility or f the market starts to go in any direction.

The most difficult part of working on pairs trading is picking out the stocks that you want to invest in. There are actually quite a few options that you can work with, but you need to make sure that you are pairing the right ones together so you make a profit as well as picking the right one to go long on and the right one to go short on. If you are able to do this successfully, you can do a great job with pairs trading.

Contrarian trading

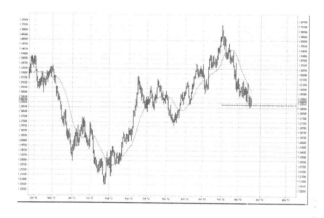

Contrarian trading is another option that you are able to use and it is going to be able to work against some of the other forms of trading that we have talked about so far. It goes against the other strategies because you are able to look at the market, and then go against it to find the assets that are performing poorly, but which you think will start to do well soon. Sometimes there are some good stocks on the market, but for some reason or another, they are not performing the way that they should. With this strategy, you would find these stocks, purchase them at a low price, and then make a profit when their value goes up.

With the contrarian strategy, you are always looking for the motive for why people tell you certain things. You are going to believe that people are telling you the market is going up are simply doing this because they invested in the stock and they don't have the option to make some other purchases. When this starts to happen, the market is near or at the peak and making the purchase is going to cost you a lot of money. On the other side of things, if you hear that the market is in a downturn, it means that the other traders already sold their stocks and the market has already gone through a downturn. This is the perfect time to make a purchase because the stock market can only go up from here.

With the contrarian trading, you go with the idea that if you follow the same path that others do, you are basically passing up on some great opportunities and you will not be able to make the income that you desire. Others have already gotten to this stock and beat you to it, so jumping on means you will just lose out because the prices are already either too high for you to purchase or too low for you to sell. With this method, you are able to fight through some of this, and pick out stocks that go against the popular trend, in the hopes that you can jump on before others purchase them, and get a great sale in the process.

Momentum trading

It is also possible to work on a strategy that is known as momentum trading. When you are using this strategy, you are going to try and predict some of the trends that could occur in the stock market prices. If you are right, you will end up making a good profit in the process. There are a couple options that you can use to guess which way the momentum is going. First, you would take the time to watch the charts on a specific stock. By looking at these charts, you are able to find some of the patterns that are going on, a back and forth between the highs and lows and when you catch this pattern, it is easier to know when to purchase and when to sell.

Now, all stocks have some kind of trend that goes with it. Some will stay high for a bit, some will stay low for a bit, and others are always going up and down. But with momentum trading, you will be able to tell what direction a stock is going to head based on where it has been recently and in the past. For example, if you notice that a stock has a pretty steady trend of going up and down, you would be able to look at one of the downward trends and guess that the price is about to go up. This would be a good time to purchase so that you get that stock at a low price and can sell it at a higher one.

This can also be used in order to help you to know when to avoid a stock or when to sell a stock you already own. If you know the trend of a stock and notice that it has stayed high for a bit, it is time to sell the stock because the price is about to go back down. This would not be a good time to purchase the stock either because unless there is going to be some big news about the company, the price of the stock will not go up, and you will end up losing money in the process.

The momentum option is going to take a look at the history and the trends of the stock and figure out which way the stock is about to go. It is a pretty secure option to use because most stocks will follow the same trends over the long term unless something drastic happens with the market. It is often best to combine this one with the news strategy so you can tell if some big event is going to change how the stocks will behave and if they are going to leave their trends, even temporarily, so you can make adjustments to what you purchase and when you sell.

Heikin-Ashi trading

When you look at the charts for this one, you will notice that it looks like the candlestick chart, but the method of plotting and calculating the candles will be a bit different compared to using the candlestick chart. On a traditional candlestick chart, each of your candlesticks will show up for numbers including the low, high, close, and open prices. But with the Heikin-Ashi candle, we are going to be able to do our candles based on some information that came from the previous candle.

Some of the things that we would look for with the Heikin-Ashi candles include:

- The close price. The Heikin-Ashi candle is going to be the average of the open, close, high, and low price.

- Open price: for this candle, it is going to look at the previous candle and look at the average of the close and open.

- The high price: for these candles, the high price is going to be chosen from one of the high, close, and open price, based on which one has the highest value.

- Low price. The high price on this candle is going to be chosen from the close, open, and high price from the previous candle that will have the lowest value.

All of the candles in this method are going to be related to each other because the close and the open price on each candle is calculated with the information from the previous candle. You will look at the open and close price of the previous candle to determine the new candle that you create.

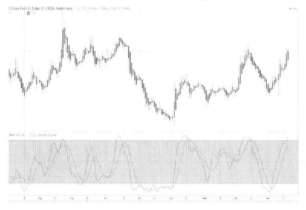

The chart above is an example of how the Heikin-Ashi candles would look. The red is going to show the bear markets, when it would be a good time to make a purchase of the stock to get it for the lowest price and the green would be the bullish markets, when it may be a good time to work on selling the stocks for a good profit.

Picking out the strategy that you are going to use when working in day trading can be really important. It is going to help you to understand how the market works, how to recognize certain signs inside of the market and to ensure that you are taking the risks that you feel the most comfortable with. All of these strategies can be successful and sometimes traders will pick a few of them to combine to get the best results. The important thing is to pick out a strategy that you feel comfortable with and then stick with that one, rather than bouncing around all the time. When you are able to do that, you will find that even as a beginner, you will be able to realize a profit.

CHAPTER 6: THE BEST PLATFORMS FOR DAY TRADERS

When starting with day trading, it is important to have the right tools. If you have the wrong broker or get started with the wrong platform, you are setting yourself up for failure from the beginning. Checking out a few different platforms will make it easier for you to start out right, helps you to avoid some of the fees that are common with some of the lower quality platforms, and can increase your money earning potential.

There are several things that you can consider when picking out a platform. The first thing to look at is the reputation of the platform, asking questions about how well they help other investors make money or if there happens to be a lot of complaints against poor customer service and high fees with this particular company. A smart investor also needs to look at the benefits that each platform brings, such as the fee structure, what types of trading they allow, and whether you get along with the broker or not before picking out the platform that you want to use.

Luckily, there are many great financial platforms you can choose to work with so you have options and can shop around to find some of the best platforms to increase your earnings.

Financial brokers in the United States

If you are working on day trading in the United States, there are many financial brokers you can choose. With that being said, there are some brokers who are able to stand above the rest of the advisors and firms based on their ease of use, knowledge about the market, and their performance. As a beginner, it may be a good idea to start with one of the following companies to help out with your day trading:

- TD Ameritrade
- Fidelity
- Charles Schwab
- E-Trade
- Merrill Edge
- Scottrade
- TradeKing
- OptionsHouse
- TradeStation
- Capital One Investing

Financial brokers in Europe

Depending on your strategy with day trading, you may find that you want to work with a financial platform based in Europe. This can also work well if you plan to expand out your portfolio and would like to work in a new market. There are some great markets to work with in Europe as well including:

- Avatrade
- XM
- LMFX
- eToro

- NetoTrade
- Markets.com
- Oanda

Picking out a good financial platform for your day trading is critical when starting your investment. When you shop around and check with a few of these brokers in order to see what services they offer, what fees they charge, and even look into their reputation to make sure you pick the platforms that meet your day trading needs.

CONCLUSION

Thank for making it through to the end of *A Beginner's Guide to Day Trading: Discover How to Be a Day Trading King.* Let's hope it was informative and able to provide you with all of the tools you need to achieve your goals of

The next step is to find a good financial broker to help you to get into the day trading market. You will find that there are many strategies that you can use, but if you find the one that helps you to think about your decisions and do the research, you are sure to see some great return on investment in the long run.

Day trading is not about gambling, it is about knowing the market and learning how to make smart decisions on when to purchase and when to sell your stocks in order to make a profit. This guidebook took the time to show you the different strategies that are successful in day trading, even for beginners. This can be a really successful choice for making a profit on your investment and this guidebook will be able to help you get started!

OPTIONS TRADING: A BEGINNERS GUIDE TO OPTION TRADING UNLOCKING THE SECRETS OF OPTION TRADING

DESCRIPTION

Trading, in general, can be confusing. Options trading can be even more confusing. This is especially true if you don't know what you are doing or if you have never dealt with trading in the past.

Just because you're a beginner, though, doesn't mean that you have to stay that way. When you read this book, you will be able to learn all of the basics that you need to help make your options trading career more successful. I can't guarantee that you will make money from options trading, but I can guarantee that this book will provide you with the tools that you need to start making money.

As you are reading through the chapters, think of the different ways that each of them applies to your situation. If you have not started building capital up yet, consider how you will be able to do that. If you have not been able to find a broker, consider that.

This book is full of ideas on how you can make sure that you are going to be the best options trader possible. Your portfolio will be filled with options trades that are good and profitable. You will also learn the basics that you need to know about hedges and even futures trading.

Are you ready to take your beginner knowledge to the next level?

INTRODUCTION

Congratulations on downloading your personal copy of *A Beginner's Guide to Options Trading*. Thank you for doing so.

The following chapters will discuss some of the many different aspects of options trading.

You will discover how important it is to make sure that you are getting a good deal on the trades that you do.

The final chapter will explore how options trading can work to give you passive income.

There are plenty of books on this subject on the market, thanks again for choosing this one! Every effort was made to ensure it is full of as much useful information as possible. Please enjoy!

CHAPTER 1: UNDERSTANDING TRADING AS A WHOLE

Trading is essentially the process of making money through smart decisions. You can buy and sell different pieces of companies and businesses, known as shares, through the process of trading. The beauty of this is that you are able to make money from it.

When you are trading, you will first start out by making an investment. This can be a large one or a small one, but most people start with just a small one so that they are not going to be out a lot of money if they happen to make a poor choice with the investment (as beginners often do). The point of trading is to have as little risk as possible when you are trading so that you will be able to keep things as profitable as possible, or break even at the very least.

After someone has initially invested in something, they will then allow it to sit for a period of time. Some people choose to just trade through the course of one day. They don't make a lot of profit at once, but they normally have many different investments that they are working with at any time. When they do this several days a week – known as day trading – the profits typically build up. Others, though, want to let their investments sit for a week, a month, a year, or sometimes even longer. When they do this, they watch the price of the investment closely and then when it is at its highest, they sell their shares for profit.

If you are planning to start trading at any point in your life, you need to know that there are differences in trading types and that you should stick to one type of trading. For example, if you have chosen options trading as your niche, you should not try to start real estate trading or investing in anything else other than what you started with.

Picking a niche is the only way that you will be able to turn into a professional. You need a niche so that you can focus on one thing. When you focus on only one thing, the experience that you gain is a lot more focused, a lot more valuable, and a lot more profitable. As a result, by working with niches, you also become a better investor.

Picking a niche like options trading is a great way to get started with trading and is something that most people will be able to handle when they are just getting started in their trading career. It is important to note that options trading isn't necessarily easy. In fact, it's not easy at all, and can be quite risky. However, it is something that you can learn in a short period of time.

If you are going to start options trading, you need to learn as much as possible about it so that you will be able to be successful at it; otherwise, you run the risk of making a poor investment and losing big. That's where this book comes in.

CHAPTER 2:OPTIONS TRADING IN A HISTORICAL SENSE

Options trading is something that is currently very popular, and it is one of the biggest forms of financial trading in the world. Billions of dollars in contracts are traded on a yearly basis, and that is something that, obviously, has a huge effect on the economy in all areas of the world. Because of this, many believe that options trading in its current form has been around for hundreds of years, but that simply isn't true.

Options trading, as we know it today, started just about 50 years ago and has ballooned since then, becoming bigger and offering more trading opportunities for people who are thus interested. Because of the risky nature and historical tendency to lead to speculative bubbles, some investors are still leery about options trading.However, modern options trading is relatively safe.As an example of how young modern options trading is, the Chicago Board Options Exchange is one of the oldest modern options exchanges and it has only been around since the 1970s.

Looking at Futures vs. Options

Futures and options are really close to being the same thing. The biggest difference lies in the way that you are able to carry out the contract. For example, you are able to sell your options at any time that you want. With futures, you have to wait until the end of the contract if you want to be able to sell the investment and start to profit off of it.

Futures are very limiting while options are very flexible in terms of selling for a profit.

Ability to Sell Your Options

One of the biggest benefits to using options is that, as I said, you can sell them at any time that you want within a certain timeframe delineated in the contract. However, this also means that you need to make sure that you are going to truly profit from the options contracts that you have established.

Because there are so many different aspects that go into trading, especially when you have somethingso functional and important as options contracts, you will be able to look at the different key points of shares and contracts,as well as the way that they are building up value while you have them. Once you've evaluated everything, if you want to sell your options and the price is at a good point, you can stand to make a huge profit off of them.

Change in the Way That Options Work

Throughout time, people recognized that there was a need to have a way to speculate on future values. Many investors liked the way that trading worked and they especially liked the way that futures worked, but they did not want to have to wait until the end of the contract to be able to profit from the trades. This was something that they always kept in mind, but it took off when options trading became a reality. There are many ways that options trading works to help enterprising investors out, and allowing them the chance to sell their investments off at anytime that they want at a certain price point gives them the flexibility that many people hope for when they are trading and when they are doing different things.

Options in the Past

Despite the fact that options are a fairly new concept in the world of modern trading, the idea behind options trading is ancient. As far back as ancient times, people were speculating on certain markets. This was something that the modern traders to base their options trading ideologies on, and it allowed them the chance to make sure that they were truly doing things the right way by comparing their set-up to the mistakes of the past, such as the Dutch Tulip bubble.

Options trading historically served the same purpose it does today: a way for people to make money off of their intuition for judging market directions. While they did not necessarily call it options trading at the time and they certainly did not have the technology that is available today, the principles behind it were the same.

Having Regulations for Options

When futures trading first started, there were a lot of regulations for it, and people had to follow each of these regulations to make sure that they were going to be able to get the best experience possible when it came to the trading opportunities. In other words, the regulations served both the investors and the economy by preventing speculative bubbles.

The same is true for options trading. However, with options trading, the regulations didn't really start to pop up until after the *concept* of options trading had been long developed. Because of this, the process for developing regulations was a little different than it had been for futures, as the process for developing regulations for options trading had been based in the historical mistakes of speculative trading.

Obviously, having the ability to look at past options trading scenarios was helpful when the regulations were being made. Looking to the past will invariably teach you a lot about the future. The same is true for options trading. There are a number of regulations in place based on the early mistakes of proto-modern options trading and early speculative markets.

In other words, the regulations for options trading may seem rather extensive, but they are as they are for very good reason.

CHAPTER 3: THE BASICS OF OPTIONS TRADING

There are a few things that you need to know before you start options trading. You need to know what options trading is, the basic language you will find in the trading world, why people choose to work with options contracts, the different orders that you can use with options trading, and the way that options work.

Definition of Options

Options are a type of trade that is in contract form. The buyer of the contract is then able to sell the asset that comes along with the contract at a specified time for a specified price. Essentially, it's a promise from one person to another to either buy or sell something at a given price, regardless of its real market price, at a certain point. The price does fluctuate both up and down when it comes to the total value of the options, as a response to the market price and the contract price. Because of this, you can be sure that you will almost always make a profit on the options if you know the right way to buy them and know the specific terms of the contract.

The biggest thing with options is that they do have an expiration date. If you do not have a chance to sell it off before that time, then you will lose your money because the contract is void.

Language You'll Hear in Options Trading

Call option – This is basically a contract in which Person A tells Person B that Person B is allowed to buy commodity/stock C at price x, regardless of market price y, as long as Person B exercises their contract by expiration date d.

Put option – The inverse of a call option; Person A tells Person B that Person B is allowed to *sell* commodity/stock C at price x regardless of market price y, as long as Person B exercises their contract by expiration date d.

Derivative – the total value of the security that comes from the purchase amount and the assets that stand underneath the total value of the contract

Expiration date – the point in which the contract will expire, and it will then not be able to make any more money. If a contract holder does not sell the contract before that time, he or she will lose out on the money that was paid for the contract.

Long position – The person who is buying an options contract is in the *long position*. They have the option, though not the obligation, to exercise the contract by a given date.

Options contract – the actual contract that is purchased as an investment. It outlines the price, the value that is going to come and the expiration date of the contract at which point it becomes completely useless to the people who have the contract and who want to be able to sell it.

Reasons for Options Trading

The two biggest reasons that most people use options trading as their main form of investment are speculation and hedging. When it comes to these two particular niches, options fill them out particularly well.

The speculation part is easy. Options trading allows you to essentially bet that stock/commodity c will rise to price y by date d. If you buy the stock/commodity c at price x, and it rises to price y – which just happens to be $10 more than price x – then you gain a total of $10 per share/unit in profit, if you turn around and sell the asset/commodity instantly at price y. You get the $10 in profit per share/unit because the options contract allowed you the ability to buy the stock/commodity c at price x even when the actual market price was y. So, with options trading, you can *assume* that an asset or commodity is going to rise in value massively for some reason or another, and then get an options contract *now* letting you buy it at a set price *later*, so that you can turn a profit simply selling the asset or commodity at market price.

Hedging, on the other hand, is one of the lowest risk tactics in options trading. The people who use hedging are able to get more out of the experiences that they have because hedging provides an assurance that their money will be safe. The options that you purchase will only be available so that you can reduce the amount of loss on your investments. If you are going to hedge with options, you need to make sure that you are doing it in combination with other stocks and trading options that you have.

How it All Works

If you have a contract that has different guarantees on it when it comes to finances, you will be able to use that contract to make sure that you are going to get more money from the various assets and commodities that you're working with. The market price of a stock that you have may be at a certain point at any one point in time. Then, the price may go up. Depending on what the options contract was written with, the price will go up with it. The contract is usually worth 100 times the rise in the stock because it is 100 shares worth of that fund.

For example, if you have an options contract that says you have 100 shares of a stock for company X, then when the price of the stock rises for company X, so does the value of your options contract. If company X goes from a value of $10 to $18, then your contract will also go up by eight points. Because you have 100 shares within that contract, it will actually be worth $800 more.

Orders for Options Trading

When you have an options contract, you will need to create some orders that will tell your broker to do specific things. These can be things like stopping the options from losing too much money or simply limiting the amount of money that gets spent on the options. If you know which order you want to use, you will be able to make sure that you are going to truly be able to have your broker do the best work possible.

Limit orders give your broker the price that you will buy or sell for.

Stop limit orders will limit the way that you are able to change your money around between different options trading contracts.

Market orders tell your broker to only act if the options stock is at a specific market price.

Stop market orders do the same as stop loss, but they are based on the market value of the options stock.

Stop loss orders are just like any other type of stop loss. You tell your broker where you want to stop losing money at.

CHAPTER 4: HOW TO GET STARTED WITH OPTIONS TRADING

One of the hardest parts of options trading is actually getting started with it. You will need to take several steps if you want to start trading and each of these steps will require you to do different things. The great part about stock options and options trading is that you will be able to use the previous starting points that you had with options trading if you ever make the decision to start a new type of trade. There are many different things that you can do when getting started out with stock options trading, and it's important that you give all of them ample thought.

Understand Your Goals

You should know what your objectives are before you start options trading. This is to help you have a clear idea of where you want to be when you are getting started, so that you can make sure that you are making all of the right options trading decisions for *you*. It can sometimes be difficult to know what you want to get out of stocks and trading.

Do you want to make a little money on the side? Do you want to replace your full-time income? Are you hoping for passive income?

Each of these things will help you to have a better understanding of the ultimate goal that you have in mind. You need to make sure that you are on the right path to get that which you want when you are looking at the different paths within an options trading career.

Try Strategies

There are several different strategies that will help you to have a better understanding of the way that options trading works. Following these strategies can be complicated at worst and stupidly simple at best. The majority of the strategies that people use for options trading are outlined in this book so that you can follow them and make sure that you are getting the best experience possible with trading.

Choose the one that best lines up with your capabilities and with the end goal that you have for your trading. If you know what you want to do with options trading and if you work to always make sure that you are getting to that point, it will be much easier for you to figure out the specific steps that you need to take while you are trading.

Always Use a Broker

Having a broker is one of the only ways to ensure that you will be able to be successful with options trading. A broker can not only help you get the best advice that you need for trades, but he or she will also help you to figure out where you need to go with each of the trades that you have. It is a good idea to try different things that the broker suggests and to make sure that you are going to be able to use these options when it comes time to trade. There are many different aspects of trading so be sure that you are paying attention to all of them.

The broker will not only be able to help you figure out what you need to do with trades and with the options contracts that you have but will also be able to help you figure out if you meet the requirements for being able to get involved in options trading.

Can You Participate?

There is a chance that you may not be eligible for options trading. About 30% of people who have the goal of options trading are not actually able to do the trades that they want to do. There are different factors that go into determining your eligibility, but the majority of them have to do with risk. If you are deemed to be high risk, if your portfolio is not large enough to satisfy the requirements, or if you show that you are somehow not able to fit options trading into your portfolio in a way that makes sense, you will not be able to participate in options trading.

Just like with other parts of trading, things can always change, though. Keep that in mind when you make the decision to try new things with options trading. You will be able to try new things, and you can even change your eligibility with time. Eligibility for options trading, indeed, is something that everyone can work toward.

Before you make the decision to invest in options trading, always check with your broker to make sure that you are eligible to do it.

The Trading Account

Once you have determined whether or not you are eligible for options trading, you will then be able to start your trading account. This is generally different from a traditional trade account in that it is a margin account. You can make sure that you are doing everything right with options contracts by starting up the margin account before you put the money into the stocks. It is a good idea to know what kind of account you are going to have and what the initial investment is going to look like for you when you start out with any sort of trading.

If you do not already have a margin account, you will need to talk to your broker about it. This is where all of the options trading actions will occur so you need to make sure that you are making a worthwhile decision about your trading account. This will essentially serve to make sure you're getting the most bang for your buck. You can also make sure that you are getting the best experience possible when your broker starts your margin account with you.

CHAPTER 5: THE DIFFERENT TYPES OF STOCK OPTIONS

There are different types of options contracts that you can choose from when you are getting started. The type of option contract that will work best for you will depend on the total capital that you have to put into the account along with the risk that you may carry. There are different things that you can choose from, and you should make sure that the options contracts that you act on line up with your goals.

Overview of Options

Options contracts largely depend upon the volatility of a stock and the amount of money which is invested. It is important to note that all of the different types of stock options can be deducted from that first initial capital function. It is a good idea to recognize that you will be able to put more money into the options stocks that you have within the contracts, but you will never have the option to lower your initial investment amount. You can always invest more but you can never uninvest without taking a potential loss.

Buying or Selling

When you are looking at the options contract that you have, it will be clear to see whether or not you are the buyer or seller. Your position will be outlined, and you will be able to figure out what the difference is between the two different parties. In each of the contracts that you have, you can only be the buyer or the seller.

For example, if you are the buyer of one contract, you will not have the opportunity to be the seller of that same contract. Instead, when you are ready to sell – and not just buy - options, you will need to make the decision to set up new contracts with assets that you already *own* (or intend to own). You can always ask your broker for assistance, here.

Striking Price

In the contract, the price is listed. The strike price is the point at which you can buy the option that is listed in the contract. It is important to note that you will not be able to buy before it reaches that price. Period.

If you are a buyer on the contract, you will also have a strike price at which you can sell. This tells you that you cannot sell until it hits the strike price. It is clear to see that this is much different from what is offered with futures. When there is a future, there is no specific strike price, but there is a strike date. The seller cannot sell before it reaches that point on the calendar. With options, you can still sell before it reaches any type of date (and you *should* sell before it hits the expiration, certainly) but you need to just be sure that it is at the right price.

The Expiration

Every single options contract will have an expiration date. This is something that must be closely monitored. For this reason, you are advised to have a broker. The broker will be able to tell you what you are doing and when the expiration date is approaching. If you find that you are getting close to the expiration date, you need to sell off the option even if your profit is not as high as what you would like it to be. If you don't, you'll lose the money that you initially put into the investment, and that can be a terrible way to start out with options trading.

Premium Investment

Your premium is basically the same as any other type of premium that you would see in investing and in stocks. It is the amount of money that you paid to purchase the options contract.

Make sure that your premium is enough to purchase the options contract but is not so much that you are going to lose a large amount of money on the trades that you are doing. You should always be careful with the stocks that you have,but options are a whole other ballpark of carefulness. Since they are somewhat of a risk, you definitely want to go for one that has a lower premium. If you do this, you will put yourself as a lower risk investment which will not only help you to lose less money but will also make you have a better appearance with your portfolio.

Style of Option

There are two main styles of options stocks.

American style – you can use the rights that you have in your contract at anytime that you have the contract in your possession. You do not have to wait until the actual expiration date so that you have more time to keep yourself from losing money. You can sell at any time after the price has hit the strike out amount.

European style – you are required to wait until the actual expiration date to be able to use that selling option. This can be a problem because it is sometimes difficult to sell a stock in one day. For example, you cannot sell the stock until you have reached the expiration date, but if you go for longer than the expiration date, you will lose out on the money that you have in your stock option contract. This is detrimental because you will not have that money that you put into the premium of the contract, so you will start out with a loss.

While the American option is the more popular among people who are trading, it is something that you will need to decide for yourself. Other than the expiration date specifics of each style, there are no major differences between the two styles of option contracts.

CHAPTER 6: CHOOSING INDEX OPTIONS

The Index Options are slightly different types of contracts, and working with them can drastically change the way that you are working with options contracts. They are simply another style that you can use when you are trading and when you have the different aspects of your trades lined up. When you choose to use an index option stock, you are simply choosing a different way that you can invest your money in the stocks that you think will be profitable.

Indexes

The most common type of index options that are available is the DJIA and the NASDAQ, which are both included in different sectors. The Dow Jones is included with companies that have very large caps on them. The initial investments, or premiums, are usually much higher with the DJIA. With the NASDAQ, you will be getting an investment that is closer to the technological side of investing, but it will cost you much less money than if you were doing it in any other way.

Choices

You can choose any sector within the two major types of indexes. This will allow you the chance to make sure that you are going to be able to get the different benefits that come with the sectors. If you are particularly interested in a sector or if you find that it is one that seems to do well according to the research that you have done, you should make that choice. It can sometimes be difficult to decide what you have done and what you are going to do in the future. If you do not know what choice you are going to make, it is wise to check with your broker. While the broker will not be able to tell you which decision you should make, he or she can give you the various beneficial points that come with each of the investments.

Advantages

The best part about the index options is that you will be able to profit in several different sectors when it comes to investing. You can get your hands into the business of many different types of investments, and that will help you to get exactly what you need with your investing opportunities. You will also be able to make more money.

The more streams of income that you have that come from investing in general, the more you will be able to profit and the more you will be able to benefit from all of the different stock price increases.

If you are going to use index options for stocks, you should make sure that you are trying more than one sector. Doing this will enable you to truly get an understanding how each of the sectors works, as well as giving you the added perk of diversified investments.

Settlement

The cash that comes from index options is the settlement amount. Since you are not actually purchasing money or investing cash in the way that you would with traditional investments, you will need to make sure that you are converting your indexes into cash. While this can sometimes be difficult to do, you need to make sure that it is something that you are prepared for. The difference in the values of the index is calculated by using the strike price. What is leftover from the strike price is what you will collect on in cash. That is what your return will be.

Capping Index

The capped index options are available to people who have options contracts. They were created so that the index option can be sold off as soon as it reaches the cap. There is no other type of trading option that gives you this type of choice. When you are making the decision to invest in options stocks, you will need to determine whether or not you want to take advantage of the capped index options and whether or not that is going to be worth the extra amount that you need to do to get to that point.

Risk Leverage

When you are looking at the risks that are associated with Options contracts and the index style of these stocks, you will need to figure out which ones are the riskiest and which ones are going to bring a low risk to you. Of course, the lower that you put the premium, the lower the risk is going to be for the stock options so you should always keep that in mind when you are looking at stock options and at the different aspects that come with them. Be sure that you are always leveraging the risks that are associated with the trades so that you can make sure that you are putting all of the options that you have in your trading portfolio.

Multiplied Contracts

When you are choosing your index options, you can get a contract multiplier. This is something that will allow you the chance to cash out on the value of the index and of the options contract that is included with the index. Make sure that you are using the options contracts that you have to be able to get the best experience possible for your trade options. Always work to provide yourself with the best trades for your portfolio and for the different things that you are adding to it.

The Premium

As with traditional options stocks, you will need to pay the premium with cash. It's sad, but true; paying premiums is an absolutely necessary part of working with options. If you are using cash for your premium, you will then be able to get the multiplier and cash in on the amount that the options stock has built up for you over the period of time that you have had it in your portfolio.

CHAPTER 7: CHOOSING CURRENCY OPTIONS

There are different trade options that will make a difference depending on the type of trade that you are doing. With options stocks, you can choose to use the index option, which is beneficial to people who do not want to deal in currency. The other option that is available, though, is currency. This is where you invest your money into the options stocks, and they are able to use the different types of currency within their own functions. This is something that is necessary if you want to be able to get the best experience possible and if you want to make sure that you are going to get your full investment back – and hopefully more.

While there are no multipliers with this type of options trade, there are different benefits that will help you to get back more cash when it comes to your trading. You do not have to worry about how much the trade value is going to change because the index does not play a part in this. You will simply have to worry about whether or not the currency that is present in these situations is fluctuating. If it is not, you can just collect on the amount that you initially put in as the financial premium.

The forex (Foreign Exchange) options provide a tool that traders and investors who are in the options contract trading business can use to make profit. They do not have to purchase the actual currency to be able to get to this point and simply have to use the leverage that they have within their portfolios so that they can make sure that they are getting the most out of the trading options available to them.

The contracts can be held when there is a currency options trade going on. This will help to reduce the amount of risk that occurs from trading and will help to prove that there will be profits from the different options that are included in all of the trades. When looking at trades, brokers and investors will both be able to see that a held contract is always a good way to reduce risk.

Choosing a currency option stock will always be lower risk than an index stock, but the payouts are often also much lower when you are using the currency trade models.

If you are using the forex model for your currency options trading portfolio, you will need to make sure that you are doing it the right way. There are different options when it comes to each of these, but they all involve the use of the forex system. If you do not want to use theforex, you will need to find a broker who does not participate in it. Brokers are not able to do forex options in addition to forex trading, because of the implications that come along with it. Investors, though, are actually able to choose two different brokers who do these things.

While there are regulations on the brokers and how they each can do the different things with the trading, there are very few on the investors when it comes to currency options trading. This is necessary for people who want to make sure that they are going to be able to get the most money possible from the trades that they are doing. It is also something that can help investors to realize what they are doing with the different trading options.

SPOT

The SPOT style of trading is intended for people who have a huge amount of startup capital they can use in order to get into forex trading. It is a high investment option and is generally not recommended for beginners, but some who have chosen it as their first options trading stock have done well with it. If you have the right broker who is able to use your stops and calls in the way that you want, you will be able to get a much better outcome from the SPOT trading option.

When you do Single Payment Options Trading, or SPOT, you will be able to bring about the different trading options. SPOT is created to automatically help you get the trades that you want. You can set up everything before you start trading and it will help you to get the payout options that you want. It will also give you the chance to be able to include all of the different aspects of trading. With SPOT, you will get a payment each time that you have made a prediction on the options trade and you are right. For those who are confident in their prediction skills, it can actually be worth the higher investment.

Call Options

The calling options that are included with the different forex styles operate almost identically to index options trading, but they are different in the sense that they involve real cash and currency that is going to change depending on the market and what is going on with the various businesses. If you know what you are doing, you will be able to call out the options and the information that is contained with each of them.

As you learn more about the call options and about the different things that are associated with the call options, you will be able to adjust the different types of options to your calling point. It is always a good idea to include the different things that are reduced with calling and putting the information into the algorithms. As you are learning more about the way that things are done in trading, the chances are that you will want to switch from this type of forex trade to one that allows you to get a single payment.

While call options are great for people who are just getting started in options trading, most usually move onto the SPOT model where they can get higher payouts for a slightly higher risk.

CHAPTER 8: ETF AND THE FUTURE OPTIONS

Just because options trading is slightly different from future trading does not necessarily mean that you can avoid everything about futures trading. It can sometimes be difficult to figure out exactly what you need to do to make sure that you are going to get each of the different options contracts to go your way; knowing more about everything related to options can help with this, including futures.

As you are looking at the options stocks, you should also consider the ETF, or exchange traded funds, along with the future options so that you can make sure that you are getting the best deal possible.

Exchange traded funds are the mutual funds of the options trading world. They are handled just like mutual funds, and they can be traded like stocks and shares are traditionally traded. If you are working with the different types of ETFs, you can look at them in the same way as mutual funds and trades.

You do not need to have a special margin account to be able to use ETFS. This is because they are available and it is legal to trade them on the regular stock exchange. You don't have to worry about the way that they are being traded or any of the implications that come along with using a smaller account or a margin account that could bring about problems in your portfolio. Always make sure that you are working with your ETFs in the same way that you would work with traditional stocks and shares.

Diversity

When you are using options trading, ETF is one of the best chances at gaining diversity in your portfolio. Since they can be traded on the open stock market, they are simple to add to your portfolio, and they can make a huge difference in the way that your portfolio looks. Always make sure that you are trying new things and that you are working to promote the different aspects of your portfolio. With ETF, you can see that there is a major difference in the way that stocks are traded in the field.

Larger Volumes

ETFs are also great if you want to have a large volume of stocks. They can be purchased in mass quantities, but the prices are generally close to the same of what a similar stock would cost you on the open market. Since they are slightly more complex than a traditional stock, they will eventually grow to be worth more than what the stocks are. This will give you the chance to see that they can be traded and they will be able to be purchased for different amounts. It is always a good idea to try out different stocks and to make sure that you have things like ETFs available in your trading portfolio so that you don't have to worry about the implications that come along with not having a diversified portfolio.

Risks

Perhaps one of the biggest benefits that come with ETFs is also their downfall. Since they are so complex, it is important to note that they cannot be used in the way that other stocks are able to be used. You must make sure that you are diversifying your portfolio heavily. Since you have them in there, you need to trade them.

If you have never had a complex stock like an ETF, you will want to check with your broker for advice on what can be done with the stock and the way that you can work to make sure that the stock is truly working for you.

Futures

Despite the fact that futures were the forerunner for options trading, they have not become completely obsolete just because options are now more prominent. In fact, there is actually a chance that futures have grown in popularity as a result of options trading. If you are hoping to diversify your portfolio even further, consider futures but also consider the implications that come with future trading options.

The Stock Exchange with Futures

Similar to options trading, you need to make sure that you have a specific margin account that was designed to be used with futures. This will help prevent you from running into major problems that could happen in the Open Stock Exchange. You cannot use futures on the stock exchange, and they will be separate from it despite the fact that the returns will be determined based on the stock exchange. Try to find the best margin fund for your futures so that you can have them separate from your options trading.

Pricing

The premium that you would typically see with a future is usually about the same as what you would see with options stocks. This is because they are very similar. Where you must wait for the date with futures, you must wait for the price with options stocks. It is a good idea to always try and make sure that you are dividing your investments evenly between the two so that, if you lose out on one, you will still have a chance to profit on the other.

Strike Dates

There is no expiration date on the futures. This is because they are meant to go infinitely unlike the options trading. There is, however, a price that you must reach before you can buy or sell the contract. That is the downside to the trades and is something that propelled the reasoning behind the options trading. It is important to know that you cannot sell unless you are at that price. You must also be able to reach a future date before you can sell. Without the expiration date, you don't have to be in such a hurry to sell, but you *do* have to wait a specified amount of time.

CHAPTER 9: OPTIONS TRADING STRATEGY TERMS

You should never jump into options trading without knowing the implications of it and the various things that you can do to make the trades better. You need to know the strategies that are available to traders, if you want to ever have a chance at making things work out within your trade portfolio. It can be easy to get caught up in the problems that come along with options trading, so make sure that you are always following the prescribed strategies so that you do not miss out on the money that you *could* be making from each of the trades.

To get the best advice on the strategies, you will need to know the terms that are used.

Bull – investor who wants to make the market asset increase. It is someone who buys up the assets and then sells them once it increases. Functions as a traditional type of investor.

Bull spread – when the bulls work to make sure that they are able to get the different things that they want in the options trading. They will often buy up several different trade options, and then they will sell them quickly. They operate as professionals and are often able to predict when there is going to be a change in the market.

Bear – completely opposite from bulls. They look for decreases in the market, and they sell off their options trades in anticipation of the drop in the price. They will then repurchase them at the lower price later on when the prices do go down.

Bear spread – the same thing as a bull spread but opposite on the level that they sell and re-buy the trades that they have worked with before.

Downside – when the hedging tool helps you to limit the loss that you have on your assets. It is often used in combination with options contracts so that you can make sure that you are getting the most out of the other types of investments that you have in your own portfolio.

Vertical – the investor wants to sell and buy at the same time. This usually does not happen exactly at the same time, but it is within a few seconds of the happening that comes along with the trades. It is necessary for investors to make sure that they are losing out on the bad deals and gaining profits on the good options trades.

Collar – another type of protection that will work similarly to hedging and will provide the investor with the security that they need when there is a huge dip in the stock market. By putting a money option into the options trade and then writing the option as if he or she were out of money, they can make sure that they are using the collar to protect themselves.

Straddle – when an investor is riding both of the options that they have. They can actually do this with more than one option, but it is usually difficult to do so especially for investors who are just starting out. They must then make a decision which one they are going to jump on and take the investment opportunity with.

Strangle – the way the investor is able to work with two completely different types of investments. The investor will do all of these different things at the same time, and the intent is for the option contracts to increase in value. Investors should know which direction each of the options are going and they should be confident in the fact that they are doing different things. If an investor does not know the direction that the investment is going in, there are implications that can often cause the investor to lose the money that they have put into the options trades.

Butterfly trading – this is similar to a vertical trade, but it is different in that itis on a much larger scale. It involves using several different options trades and making sure that they are being simultaneously sold and purchased at the same time. An investor will do this if he or she thinks that there is going to be a big change in the market. By selling and buying at the same time, he will set himself up for the changes that are going to come in the market, and it will make things much easier when the change *does* happen to the market – whether it is a drop or a rise in the price.

If you are able to look at each of these terms and know what they mean in a grander sense, you are then ready to move onto the next chapter. If you feel that you are still not familiar with them, study them and apply them to real world situations.

The easiest way to practice the terms, learn what they mean, who they apply to, and the way that you can use them on your own is to create a practice scenario. Figure out the trading scenario that you want to come up with and label each of the parts of it. If you are confident with your trading terms, you should then try to learn the different aspects of the trades and what they will mean to you.

It is always a good idea to make sure that you are familiar with the basic terminology because that is just the starting point.

While these terms are helpful and they can create a better outlook for you while you are investing, you will be able to learn much more when you start the true trading process. You will quickly find that these are just a starting point and that there are so many more points that you will need to keep track of when you are doing different things in the trading field. Always learn as much as you can and make note of it. Consider keeping these terms handy so that you can use them later on.

CHAPTER 10: THE OPTIONS TRADING STRATEGY

Learning the different types of strategies that are available to you will help you to make the right choice when it comes time for you to start trading and getting the profits that you desire from the trades that you make. It is a good idea to be sure that you know which strategy is going to work for you based on the goals that you have set up for yourself. When you are working to make sure that you are choosing the right type of strategy, you can figure out which options line up with the goals that you have and how you want to involve all of the different aspects.

Long Position

People who want to buy a lot before the price increases generally use this type of strategy. If you want to create a large profit over a long period of time, you can take advantage of having a long position available to you.

Since you can base your position off of the leverage that you are going to get from the trading options, you will be able to use the leverage to your advantage. If you have a very strong portfolio, the long position will work the best with you.

If you are going to invest your money, consider doing so with the $5,000 model in the shares that you are going to use. If the average price of the shares is $127, you can get 39 shares out of the company. If you want to add just a bit more money, you can get the full 40 shares out of the company. If the shares go up over the period of time that you have them in, your shares' value will go up, too. When you are investing in the shares, you need to keep in mind that it sometimes takes a long time to get a return on the shares. In the short time that the shares went up by just a few dollars, you would have profited only around $120. If you wait just a little longer, the shares will probably rise again, and you will be able to profit even more from the initial investment that you made. The long position takes patience and time, but it is often worth it if you want to get the highest profits possible.

Short Position

You can purchase the stocks for a short position if you do not want to risk a lot of money. Wait until the price goes way down before you buy them and then allow yourself the chance to purchase them at a low price. Before they drop again, sell them. This would make you a bearish type of trader in a market that is bullish. You can try different things with short positioning, but you will almost always profit more if you can sellthe shares for a profit quicker. After you have sold them (before the decrease), you should wait until the decrease happens. When it does, use the profit that you received from selling them and then buy them back up again. Do this over and over again until the market stops decreasing.

Most of the people who are taking options trading approaches for the first time will generally use this type of strategy. It is safer than long positioning, it brings profits in right away, and it makes it easier for people to be sure that they are going to get the best return possible for the trades that they have. It is also something that will show you how much money you *can* make from options trading so that it will give you a boost at the beginning.

Calling Covers

If you combine the short and the long positions together, you will get the strategy that most people use once they are comfortable with both short and long. You should first learn the short position. Next, take a bull approach and try to use the long position. From there, you can combine them both. Buy stocks when they are very low and hang onto them until they are very high. Sell them off before the decrease and then repurchase them so that you can make sure that you are making money when they are at the lowest amount possible. If you want to be able to get the best experience possible with your trading, you will be able to learn both short and long positioning.

There is not a single investor out there who is successful and who only uses either short or long positioning. All of the best investors will be able to use both of them in combination with each other so that they can make sure that they are getting the best experience possible. It is necessary for investors to make sure that they are going to be able to do everything that they can when it comes to their position.

Protection

There are times when you may come across options trades that seem like they are going to be risky. You may see that their returns are going to be great but the initial investment is very risky and something that you will have to weigh against the potential benefits. If you go for this risky sort of investment, consider the protection that comes with it.

Similar to how you use options stocks to create a hedge for your traditional trading, you can also use hedges for the options stocks. This will help you to make sure that you are protected and that you are going to be able to be as protected as possible from any negative ramifications. You can be unafraid to take risks that are associated with trading when you know that you have a hedge in place that can protect you. Be sure that you do this when you know that the rewards are going to be better than what some of the risks are. Your financial protective structures will help to balance the weight with the problems.

Chapter 11: Ensuring Success

with Options Trading

There is no way to guarantee that you are going to be successful 100% of the time with any type of trading, especially options trading. The idea behind options trading is that it is slightly riskier than any other type of trading, but on the other hand, if you do it the right way, you will witness some of the largest returns you will ever see across any form of trading. The general idea in the world of finance is that the amount of risk is correlative to the amount of reward. This is true even with options trading. It may be hard to figure out the right way to do it but following each of these tips will guarantee that you have given yourself a chance to make money from the trades that you have initiated.

Build Capital

Before you start investing in any way, you need to build up capital. You cannot expect to have good returns on an investment if it is just a small amount. While you may be very proud of yourself for having 100 dollars in your bank account, the bad news is that this is just not enough to get started with investing. If you want to be able to even come close to purchasing worthwhile options contracts, you will need far above $1,000 to get started. You can get cheaper ones... but the thing is that those contracts are cheap for a reason.

Keep saving, and you will, eventually, have the money that you need to invest. By the way, are you using a high-interest savings account to save that money? You should be!

Wise Investment

No matter what type of options trade you are going to get involved in, you need to make sure that the investment is one that makes sense. Do all of the required research on the company before you invest your money into it. If you don't do this, you will risk not getting the return that you want from the investment. An investment is an *investment*. Why would you invest into something that you know nothing about? You will probably struggle at first when it comes to all of the different aspects of options trading, and you may find starting out that it's even a bit overwhelming. However, always try your best and keep a close eye on the different market approaches to trading. Wisdom comes solely from experience.

Take (Some) Risks

There are always going to be risks with trading. Whether they are risks dealing directly with your capital supply or risks dealing more specifically with your different investitures is dependent upon how good of a trader you are. Be sure that you work hard to take the right kind of risks and that you are taking the right kind of chances. You should learn what you are comfortable with when it comes to the risks that you are going to take. How much do the benefits outweigh the risk? Is the benefit big enough that it will be worth it if you lose the money that you put into the investment? If your answer is no, you probably should not take the risk.

Adjust Your Positioning

If you find that you are struggling to get the positioning right with your investment, you should change it. This does not mean that you will make a huge switch from a long position to a short position or the other way around, but it does mean that you will need to make sure that you are going to get the best return possible from wherever you are. Take specific and special pains to write down how you are performing from both the short and long positions. Consider the results. Do you consistently perform badly in the long position? Look at what's happening in those trades – every aspect – and see where things are going wrong. In the end, if you are finding that your position isn't working, just try your best to change it and to make sure that you will be able to include different options with the positions that you initially set out to take.

Re-Invest the Money

When you make money, you need to reinvest that money. With the money just sitting there, you are not going to be able to earn more on it. Since you have the money in the first place, take the smallest amount of profit off of it to pay yourself and then reinvest the rest of the money so that you can, quite simply, use your profits in order to turn more profits.

Broker Experience

When you are shopping for a broker, make sure that the broker who you are going to work with has experience in options trading. There may be brokers who have years of experience on the open stock exchange, but they may not have any idea about the options trading sector. This can mean different things for different people, but it is always a good idea to make sure that you get pertinent and up-to-date information from your broker. If your broker *does* have experience with options trading, make sure that it is the kind of experience that you are looking for and that it is something that you can use to make your trading options more professional. This is especially important if you have never traded before and if you want to get the best trading profits possible. Does your broker have a positive history with the options trading sector? Do what you can to find out.

Don't Put All Your Eggs In One Basket

Make sure that you are trying different types of options trades. If you have a lot of money to invest, don't invest it all in one type of options trading. Instead, invest it in several different options contracts that seem like they would be a good fit for your portfolio. Always do your best to ensure that you are choosing *good* options contracts and that the trades that you have are ones that will make the most sense for you and your portfolio.

Consider the Payout

You need to keep the end game in mind each time that you try to invest in different things. The end game, of course, is the payout that you are going to be able to get when you exercise an options contract. If you are looking for different options that are within your trading budget, you will need to make sure that you are doing everything that you can to include these new potential option contracts.

Try Something New

Trying new things is a great way to ensure that you are going to be able to get the highest profit possible. If you are not aware of the different profits that come from different trade options, you – quite simply – are just going to remain inexperienced and won't ever become a masterful options trader. Each time that you decide to invest again, take a look around. Take into account all of the information available to you about every single stock on the various markets that you're looking at.

CHAPTER 12: IS PASSIVE INCOME POSSIBLE WITH OPTIONS TRADING?

Many people look for passive income. They put a lot of work into their trading in the beginning so that they do not have to do as much later on and so that they can make sure that they are going to continue profiting for years to come. What most people don't know, though, is that it is actually difficult to gain passive income from things like options investing.

Set It Up

You can prepare for passive income by always setting up your options trading with the things that you want it to do. You should have a good idea of the way that it works and the different things that you can do with options trading before you try to step back and away from the different things that happen in trading. You can expect to be options trading for at least five years before you know the different things that will set you up for passive income success. When you have done this, and you are constantly recycling the money that you have made back into the investments, you will know that you are ready to try to make passive income.

You Need a Broker

While you should have a broker who is helping you with your options trading already, you will need a broker who will be able to help you run the whole operation. This can be the regular broker that you have been using the whole time or it can be someone new who specializes in the type of passive income that you want to be able to make. If you find a good broker who is also able to help you with your passive income goals, you should rely on that one to do it for you when you try to make passive income.

Automation

There are certain things that you can use in order to automate the trading process. This will not work all of the time if you are doing options trading, but you can make sure that you have certain safeguards in place that will allow you to make passive income. The whole process cannot be completely automated – that's what your broker is for – but automation *is* something that will take a lot of the pressure off of the whole affair of options trading. Computers are, in some ways, smarter than people. They can be programmed to make the best decisions and every computer error is simply a human error coming back down the line.

Use Stops

Stop losses, limits, and protocols can all be put in place to ensure that you don't lose *too* much money. This means that you will need to figure out the right way to do each of these things and that you will need to include all of these different things with your assets and options trading. Always make sure that your broker knows where you want to stop the loss or limit the trades at so that you don't lose all of the money that you have built up in the time leading up to when you started to take a more hands-off approach to the deals.

In closing, yes, you can make passive income with options trading. It is not easy, though, so you may want to just keep doing options trading on your own and profiting off of it in that way. If you'd like to make passive income off of it though, it is most certainly possible. You need a very good and competent broker behind you, too.

CONCLUSION

Thank for making it through to the end of *A Beginner's Guide to Options Trading.* Let's hope it was informative and able to provide you with all of the tools you need to achieve your goals of making money through the various options trading sectors.

The next step is to start saving up your money or to head out on your search for the perfect broker who will help you learn as much as you can about the trades that will one day make you rich.

DAY TRADING: STRATEGIES ON HOW TO EXCEL AT DAY TRADING

DESCRIPTION

Day trading is an incredibly competitive field, but there is undoubtedly money to be made there if you know what you are doing. Unfortunately, even if you are familiar with what works in the stock market, you may not be prepared for the unique life of the day trader which is why it is helpful to have as many proven strategies up your sleeve as possible. If you have already dipped your toe into the waters of day trading and are looking to take your skills to the next level then *Day Trading: Strategies on How to Excel at Day Trading* is the book you have been waiting for.

Inside you will find a detailed breakdown of many of the most common patterns that are the secret to success for a wide range of day trading strategies whether you want to focus on the 1-minute chart, the 5-minute chart or even the 4-hour or daily charts. While many day traders focus on making as many trades as possible, the truth is that quality is just as important as quality, if not more, so and *Day Trading: Strategies on How to Excel at Day Trading* can show you how to only find the best trades while blocking out the rest of the market's noise.

While day trading is often placed on a pedestal by those who haven't yet mastered its ins and outs, the truth of the matter is that it is just like any other type of trading at its heart. If you can learn the strategies, and you have the mental fortitude to act only when your indicators tell you it's time and always get while the getting is good, then you can be a successful day trader. All you need is the strategies in this book to help you on your way.

So, what are you waiting for? Get ready to take control of your financial future and live the life you've always wanted! Get started now and buy this book today!

Inside you will find

- 14 different patterns that will help you determine the current momentum of the market no matter what the specifics.

- The 6 different types of gaps and how to make the most out of each of them before the fills set in.

- 8 different patterns and strategies for trading reversals to ensure you are always prepared to make the most from market movement.

- Everything you ever wanted to know about rising and falling wedges as well as the mysterious sideways wedge.

- *And more...*

INTRODUCTION

Congratulations on downloading *Day Trading: Strategies on How to Excel at Day Trading* and thank you for doing so. Day trading is an incredibly competitive field, but there is undoubtedly money to be made there if you know what you are doing. Unfortunately, even if you are familiar with what works in the stock market, you may not be prepared for the unique life of the day trader which is why it is helpful to have as many proven strategies up your sleeve as possible.

As such, the following chapters will discuss many of the most widely used day trading strategies to ensure you are on a level playing field when you head out to meet the competition. First you will learn about the benefits of momentum trading including the anatomy of momentum stocks, the right entry points and the right screeners to use to find them as well as the filters to use to make them worth your time. You will also learn several relevant chart patterns and multiple different strategies to take advantage of them as completely as possible.

Next you will learn all about strategies for trading the gap including all the different types of gaps, what it takes to fill them and strategies to profit from them before they are lost completely. You will learn strategies for trading full gaps, partial gaps and everything in between. Then you will learn all about reversals and how to put them to use for you. You will learn how to expertly identify a reversal and how to take what you have found and profit from it via a variety of different patterns and strategies.

Finally, you will learn all about wedge patterns and how to put them to work for you. You will learn about rising, falling and sideways wedges, what each means and the strategy that will work best in each situation. When you are finished you won't be able to look at a chart without seeing something that you can make a profit from.

There are plenty of books on this subject on the market, thanks again for choosing this one! Every effort was made to ensure it is full of as much useful information as possible, please enjoy!

CHAPTER 1: MOMENTUM
TRADING STRATEGY

Simply put, momentum is what day trading is all about. This is because the only way you are ever going to find a profit while day trading is by finding the stocks that are moving the most in any given day. Luckily, each day, it is not unrealistic to assume that you will be able to find at least one stock that will move as much as 30 percent. The stocks that makes these types of moves tend to all share a few common technical indicators.

Anatomy of momentum stocks

High momentum stocks will all typically share several things in common, so much so that, when given a list of 5,000 stocks, you can typically narrow the list down to 10 or less per day.

Float: First and foremost, you are going to want to look for those that have a float of less than 100mil shares. Float refers to the total number of shares that are currently available. Float can be determined by taking the total number of outstanding shares and subtracting from it the number of shares that are currently closely-held as well as those shares that are restricted. Shares that are closely-held are those that are owned by employees, major shareholders and insiders. Restricted stock shares are those that are held by insiders and are currently under a lock-up period or other temporary restriction. The smaller the float, the more volatile the stock is likely to be. Small float also indicates low liquidity and a greater ask-bid spread.

Strong daily charts: It is important that the stocks you chose are consistently above their moving averages and are trending well away from any potential support or resistance depending on if you are following an upward or a downward trend.

Substantial Relative Volume: Ideally, you will want to be on the lookout for stocks that are at least twice what the current average is. The average you are comparing to will be the current volume versus the historical average for the stock in question. Standard volume resets every night at midnight so this is a great indicator for which stocks are seeing the most action in the moment.

Fundamental catalyst: While not required, you may also find it helpful to choose stocks that are currently gaining a momentum boost from external sources. Things like activist investors, FDA announcements, aggressive public relations campaigns and earnings reports are all likely to jumpstart momentum.

Strong exit indicators

In addition to knowing what a viable stock to trade based on momentum looks like, is also important to know when you are going to want to get out to ensure you don't lose the profit you have made. Keep the following in mind and you will be able to hold onto all your hard work more reliably.

When you hit your profit target: If you hit the profit target you were aiming for them the best choice is to sell off half of your holdings and then adjust your stop loss to account for the potential for additional gains.

Red candles: If you haven't yet reached your profit target, if a candle closes out red then you should take this as an indicator to exit. If you have already sold off half of your holdings then you are going to want to hold through this first red candle as long as it doesn't trigger your stop loss

Extension bar: An extension bar is a candle with spike that causes dramatically increased profits. If this occurs you want to lock in your profits as quickly as possible as it is unlikely to last very long. This is your lucky day and it is important to capitalize on it.

Find the right screener

In order to use a momentum strategy successfully, you are going to need to use a reliable stock screener to find stocks that are trending towards the extreme ends of the market based on the above criteria. Screeners are an indispensable tool when it comes to narrowing down field of stocks that are right for you on any given day. The best screeners allow you to add in your own filters and then only display the stocks that meet all of the criteria determined. The following is a list of the most popular free screeners on the market today.

StockFetchter.com: StockFetcher can be a little complicated, but those who take the time to learn its ins and outs agree that it is one of the most powerful screeners on the market today. This power is due to its practically unlimited number of custom parameters and filters which allow you to create your own screens. The free version of this service will then allow you to see the top 5 stocks that match your criteria which is often enough to find a few worthwhile trades each day. There is also an upgraded version which will show you all of the available results for just $8.95 per month.

Finviz.com: Finviz offers thousands of premade filter combinations to return results on the most promising stocks for a given day. The tool is extremely easy to use as it offers three main drop-down menus, technical, descriptive and fundamental, and lets you choose one or more criteria from each. Results can then be sorted in 14 different ways to ensure you can always find the stocks you are hoping for. Be aware, however, that Finviz uses delayed data which makes it most effective for those who run their screens in the evenings in preparation for the next day's open.

Chartmill.com: Chartmill allows you to filter stocks based on standard criteria such as candlestick patterns, technical indicators, volume, price and performance. It also offers proprietary filters including things like trend intensity, squeeze plays and pocket pivots. Chartmill works via a credit system and provides each user with 6,000 credits per month free. Each scan then costs a few hundred credits which means most users can take advantage of their tools free of charge. Additional credits cost $10 per 10,000 or they have an unlimited option available for about $30 per month.

Stockrover.com: Stockrover is a useful tool if you are interested in trading in the Canadian market as well as the US market. It utilizes fundamental filters along with those that are performance and technical based. This tool allows you to track stocks that are near established highs and lows, those that are gaining momentum and even those that are currently being traded by major hedge funds. It also allows you to create custom screens and to create equations for more advanced screening. It then allows for backtesting to ensure the equations are up to snuff. Most of their options are available to free users but some features are gated behind a price tag of $250 per year.

Choosing the right filters

As a day trader, you are going to want to not only find stocks that have a high volume, but those that are currently experiencing a high degree of movement as well. In order to find the stocks that are going to see the greatest degree of movement, consider the following filters.

Constant volatility: In order to trade the most volatile stocks with the least amount of research try the following list of criteria in your favorite screener that allows for personalized screens. While more research is always better, you can even see success running this screen once a week and then trading the results for the coming week.

- show stocks where the average day range (50) is above 5%
- and price is between $10 and $100
- and average volume (30) is greater than 4000000
- and exchange is not Amex
- add column average volume (30)
- add column average day range (50)

This criterion will then return stocks that, over the past 50 days, have moved at least 5 percent each day. It is important to use at least 50 days, though

75 or 100 are going to produce even more reliable results. This shows that a given stock has moved a significant amount repeatedly over the past few months. The second criterion determines the amount you are willing to pay per share and can be altered based on your specific needs.

The next criterion determines the amount of volume you are looking for in a given timeframe. The example looks for volume over 4 million shares in the past 30 days. Next, this criterion eliminates leverage ETFs from the results which can be eliminated if you are interested in trading ETFs. Finally, the add column will show a list of the stocks with the largest volume and the greatest amount of movement. Selecting these columns will rank the results from lowest to highest based on the provided criteria.

Monitor daily to find the biggest moves: Alternately, you may prefer to search every day for the stocks that are likely to experience the greatest range of movement. To do so, you will want to create a new list of stocks each evening so that you are ready to go for the next morning when the market opens. This list can be made up of stocks that have a high volatility during the preceding day, either the greatest percentage of gains or losses. Adding in volume criteria will then help to make sure the results will continue to generate the kind of volume day trading requires. Useful filters for this search include an average volume of greater than 1 million, the greater the volume, the fewer results you will see.

When using this strategy, it is important to take note of the well-known stocks that are likely to see news release as these can often cause price movement that is unpredictable unless the details are already known. It is best to wait until after these releases have gone public to begin your trades as this is likely when both volatility and volume will be at their highest point. If you don't have your own, the earnings calendar found at Yahoo! Finance is a great place to start.

Intra-Day volatility monitoring: Another viable option is to do your research during the day to determine the stocks that are experiencing the highest degree of movement. Most trading platforms provide this information in real time. This makes it easy to keep abreast in changes that occur throughout the day. As an example, if a stock opens at a point down 10 percent from its previous close and stays there, then you know there isn't any trading happening there. However, if it starts at 10 percent down and keeps dropping then you can start considering it for a potential trade. You may also find it useful to track stocks that are currently breaking their established resistance levels.

Find the biggest moves: In order to find the stocks that are very likely to make big moves without committing to constant research, you will want to focus on stocks that are proving to be constantly volatile. This is another scan that can be run over the weekend to prepare for the week ahead. Alternately, you can run this scan each evening and monitor the differences daily instead. Additionally, you may want to monitor volatility during the day to determine which stocks have been the most active during the current session.

Double check the details with chart patterns

After you have found a stock or 3 that your scanner of choice says is likely to move with the momentum you are looking for, the next step is to double check that information. This means you are going to want to start by reviewing its candlestick chart and try to determine the correct entry point based on the first pull back. It is common for traders to simply buy at the point of pull back which then creates an additional spike in volume which pushes the stock price up further. Finding the best entry point in real time is key to long-term success as a day trader.

Pennant: A pennant forms when there is significant movement in a given stock followed by a consolidation period which causes the pennant shape created by a pair of converging lines. A breakout is then likely to occur in the same direction as the previous movement. There will likely be significant movement at first, followed by weaker volume as the tip of the pennant forms, followed again by strong growth and additional volume after the breakout.

Cup and handle: The cup and handle pattern looks like the bowl of a cup with the ride side handle. The pattern is u-shaped, charting a series of lows for the stock while the handle also slopes slightly downward. This is a sign that volume is going to remain low overall and that the stock in question should be avoided.

Ascending triangle: This pattern typically forms during an upward trend and indicates that the current pattern is going to continue. It is a bullish pattern that says greater growth and volume are on the way. It can also be formed during a reversal, signaling the end to a downward trend.

Triple bottom: The triple bottom, named for the 3 bottoming out points of a given stock, tends to indicate that a reversal is on the way. You can tell a triple bottom by the fact that the price rebounds to the same point after each period of bottoming out. After the third period, it is likely to reverse the trend by breaking out.

Descending triangle: This is similar to the ascending triangle but is bearish rather than bullish. It indicates that the current downward trend is likely to continue. It can occasionally be seen during a reversal but is much more likely to be a continuation.

Inverse head and shoulders: The inverse head and shoulders consists of 3 low points always returning to the same higher price. The lowest point is considered the head while the shoulders are a pair of low points that are equal to one another. After the second shoulder, a breakout is likely to occur that will pick up volume as it goes.

Bullish triangle: This is a symmetrical triangle pattern that can be easily determined by a pair of trendlines that converge at a point. The lower trendline tracks support while the upper tracks resistance. Once the price breaks through the upper line then you know that a breakout has occurred that will rapidly pick up both steam and volume.

Rounded bottom: This pattern tracks a prolonged drop in price that will eventually rebound back to the point where it started. After the rebound occurs a reversal and breakout is likely to occur though it is best avoided as the new trend is likely not going to be strong enough to suit your day trading purposes.

Flag continuation: This pattern forms a rectangle with the support and resistance lines remaining parallel to one another. The slope of the parallel is likely to move counter to the original price movement. The point where the price breaks through can signal a strong indicator to buy or sell based on the direction of the breakout.

Bearish triangle: This triangular pattern is easy to identify because the support and resistance lines converge in a downward slope. The breakout point is always going to be on the support side and indicates a strong downward trend is forming that is likely to pick up volume significantly as it goes along.

Falling pennant: This pattern looks a lot like a triangle pattern except it doesn't quite come to a point. The trendlines will connect several peaks and valleys and once the breakout occurs it is likely that the price will move sharply in the direction of the breakout.

Double top: This pattern involves a pair of trendlines that are a good distance apart that track a price through a pair of significant downward movements that both return to the same high point in between. Once the price breaks through the support line then you can count on significant downward movement in the near future.

Head and shoulders (standard): This is the opposite of the inverse head and shoulders discussed above. It is created by three distinct price points, one at a higher point than the other two which all return to the same low point in the interim. The breakout will eventually come at the support line and will indicate the start of a new downward trend.

The importance of the bull flag: Of the patterns that you are likely to run across most frequently, the bull flag pattern may well be the most important. It is a flag that you are likely to run into every day and it provides the ability to enter at a low risk point on otherwise very strong stocks. With this pattern, you are going to want to look for an entry point after the first candle that creates a new high after the breakout has already occurred. To find this pattern, you simply keep an eye out for stocks that are squeezing up and forming tall candles. You then wait until these have formed 2 or 3 pullback candles.

The first candle to perform positively after this occurs is where you will enter, while placing a stop loss at the low point of the pull backs. It is important to get in quickly after the candle high point as right after this the volume typically spikes dramatically.

Other things to keep in mind

Setting stops properly: When it comes to day trading you always want to keep a 2 to 1 profit/loss ratio. As such, you are typically going to want to set a tight stop that is just below the first pullback point of the stock in question. A good profit target is typically 40 cents per share, which means that you are often going to want to set your stops 20 cents lower than your target. If the stop is greater than 20 cents then you may want to manually end the trade and come back for a second try. This is a good strategy because generating stops at greater than 20 cents means you quickly need to make $1 or more per trade which can be harder than it might first seem.

You will find that it is much easier to find success with 40 cents worth of profit as opposed to setting a stop of $1 and trying to make $2 of profit, the day trading market is simply too volatile for this to be successful in most instances. Your goal here should be to balance your level of risk across the entire time you spend trading. The easiest way to calculate the specific risk of a given trade is to determine the distance between the entry point and the stop. If you have a stop set at 20 cents and want to ensure the total risk is no greater than $500 then you will be able to worry about 2,500 shares at a time.

Ideal time to trade: While you can use momentum trades successfully at any time between 9:30 am and 4 pm, you will typically find them most successful between 9:30 am and 11:30 am. With that being said, if there is an incoming news release it will likely be worth your time to trade once it has been announced, regardless of the time of day. After 11:30 am, you will likely have the best results working from the 5-min chart exclusively. The 1-minute chart typically becomes much choppier after 11:30 am which can make it difficult to set stop losses effectively.

Analyze your results: Trading successfully in the long term is all about statistics which means you are going to want to keep an eye on your success/loss ratio every day to ensure that you are always moving in the right direction. At the end of each week you are going to want to determine your current trading metrics. If you have a month's worth of subpar metrics then you are going to want to take a serious look at your trading strategy and determine what you can do to change it for the better.

CHAPTER 2: TRADING THE GAP

Gap trading strategies are a set of strictly regimented systems of trading that focus on a narrow band of criteria to determine profitable entry and exit points. Gap trading is a fairly simple process as you don't need to worry about bottoms or tops but the range as a whole. While the process is simple, the execution can be rather difficult and it is recommended that you practice before putting it to work in a big way.

A gap is the physical evidence of differing price levels between the end of the preceding day and the start of the next day. In general, the size of the gap in question can provide you with plenty of information when it comes to the strength of the gap as well as its location. When combined with additional information related to price action and technical analysis you can gain greater insight when it comes to the psychology and dynamics that caused it.

While trading based solely on the size of a gap can lead to a mixed bag of trade results, when used as part of a whole it can be a very helpful way to find the types of trades you are looking for as a day trader. The main types of gaps are outlined below. Keep in mind that, while the type of gap can help you learn about price dynamics, market sentiment and momentum, they are still lagging indicators. They can only be classified after the fact once the price has moved on.

Breakaway gap: This type of gap is used to describe a situation where the price of a given stock either gaps over a resistance or support level. This type of price gap often leads to breakouts and additional bullish movement.

Exhaustion gap: This scenario typically forms after a substantial trend has already occurred. It is generated when the price makes one final jump in the direction of the prevalent trend and then reverses dramatically.

Common gap: As the name indicates, a common gap is the most frequently seen gap which occurs without typically indicating much of anything when it comes to overall movement. Common gaps occur most frequently when the price of a given stock is ranging. They are typically not very large and, as such, tend to fill in quite quickly.

Continuation gap: This situation most frequently takes place in a trend that is already taking place. If it occurs during an uptrend then it indicates the trend is likely to continue as it marks the point that additional buyers jumped into the market, pushing the price to greater heights in the process. The same can be said for a downward trend and new sellers entering the market.

Full gap: This type of gap frequently occurs when the price at the open of the current day is dramatically different than that of the previous day. It occurs as a positive if a starting price of a given stock is greater than the high point that price reached sometime the day before. Likewise, a negative full gap appears if the starter price is below the lowest point from the previous trading day.

Partial gap: This type of gap occurs when there has been a moderate amount of change between the price between yesterday at close and today's open. A partial gap up occurs when the price at open is greater than yesterday's price at close, but is not greater than the previous day's high. A partial gap down occurs when the price at open is lower than yesterday's close, but not greater than yesterday's overall low.

Fills

When a gap is filled, it returns to the price point of its pre-gap self. Fills are always going to happen because the market prefers a stable state. When a gaps is filled within the same trading day as the gap came into existence this is referred to as fading. As an example, consider a company announces a positive news release at the end of a business day, causing a significant gap to form the following morning. As the day progresses, investor realize the news release was largely smoke and mirrors which would shift the stock from heavily bought to heavily sold. Once the price returns to yesterday's close level the gap is filled. Fills are manifested due to several different factors, including:

Technical resistance: When the price of give stock generates a gap, the price moves in a given direction so sharply that it doesn't create any new support or resistance. This gives it nothing to push against for future moves which means it takes less effort by the market to get things back to where they started from.

Irrational exuberance: Irrational exuberance occurs when investor enthusiasm reaches such a fevered pitch that it pushes stock prices to levels that aren't supported by any fundamentals. A historical example of irrational exuberance is the fervor in which the stock for internet companies were traded during the later 1990s. Spikes of irrational exuberance can be positive or negative and often leave significant gaps in their wake due to the speed at which buyers or sellers jump onto a given stock.

Price pattern: Price patterns will help you to classify gaps, making it easier to determine how quickly they are going to be filled in. Exhaustion gaps are the ones that are likely going to be filled in first as they always signal the end of an existing trend. Breakaway gaps and continuation gaps are likely to fill in much slower as they indicate the continuation of an existing trend.

Full gap strategies

The primary tenet of gap trading is to give the market 1 hour to establish a range in the stock price. After a full gap position has been entered into you will want to set a trailing stop that is 8 percent for long positions and 4 percent for short positions.

As an example, if you are going long on a particular gap which follows a stock that is currently trading at $100 then you would want to set a trailing stop at $92. If the price increases to $120 then you will want to increase the stop to $110.375. The stop will then keep rising as long as the price does the same. If you short a stock that is currently worth $100 then you will want to set a buy to cover at $104 so that a trend reversal would force an exit after 4 percent movement. If the price then drops down to $90 you would change the stop to a buy to cover of $93.

Full gap up long: If the opening price of a given stock opens above the previous day's high point then you are going to want to take a look at the short timeframe charts post 10 am. You will then want to set a long stop that is two ticks higher than the high point of the first hour of trading. In this instance, a tick is the spread of the bid/ask price which is typically between ¼ and 1/8 depending on the stock in question.

Full gap up short: If the stock price movement creates a gap but then fails to sustain the rise with sufficient buying power then the price of the stock in question will either drop below the price of the gap at open or level out. When this occurs, you will want to take advantage of it by setting short position entry signals. This means you will want to look at the 1-minute shortly after 10:30 am and set a short stop that is two ticks lower than the lowest point that was seen in the first trading hour.

Full gap down long: News of organizational changes, poor earnings, a news release with ill tidings and other market influences can all cause the price of a specific stock to drop dramatically at the start of the trading day. When a full gap down occurs at the open and then starts to climb dramatically from there, it is known as a "dead cat bounce". In order to take advantage of this position you are going to want to set a long stop at a point that equals two ticks more than the low of the previous day.

Full gap down short: If the opening price of a given stock is below the low then you are going to want to look to the short timeframe charts post 10 am before create a short stop that is equal to two ticks less than the lowest price point achieved during the first hour of trading.

Partial gap strategies

When it comes to trading partial gaps as opposed to full gaps, the biggest differences are the amount of potential gain when compared to the overall risk. As a general rule, a stock that presents a full gap has created enough of a change that the market will naturally desire to buy or sell it depending on the direction of the gap. Demand is going to be large enough to force a change. As such, the trend of full gaps tends to be much greater than those of partial gaps.

For partial gaps, the demand will naturally be smaller as well, which will require less price fluctuation to satisfy the demand. Partial gaps fill in more quickly as interest wains after the initial round of trade orders which causes the stock to return to the regular range. As such, in order to be successful with partial gap trades you will need to keep a closer trailing stop of around 5 or 6 percent as well as pay closer attention to the price movement.

Partial gap up long: If the opening price of a given stock is above the close from yesterday but does not quite reach its high, then you are dealing with a partial gap up. To take advantage of this fact you are going to want to look to the short timeframe charts post 10 am before setting a long stop that is roughly about 2 ticks over the high that was achieved during the first hour of the day.

Partial gap up short: In order to take advantage of a partial gap up by shorting you will want to look towards short timeframe charts post 10 am before setting a buy stop that is two ticks above the highest price that was achieved during the first trading hour of the day.

Partial gap down long: If the opening price is lower than the close of the previous day but not quite to that day's overall low, then you are going to want to look to the short timeframe charts post 10 am before setting a buy stop that is two ticks higher than the high point of the previous trading hour.

Partial gap down short: If the opening price for a given stock is below the close point of the previous day but not to that day's overall low then you will want to look to the short timeframe charts post 10 am before setting a short stop that equals approximately 2 ticks less than the low for the first hour of trading that day. If the stock doesn't meet the required level of volume in the meantime you will want to wait until the price breaks past the previous high, for longs, or low, for shorts, and then get out as soon as possible as the trend is unlikely to last.

Other gap trading methods

End of day gap trading: All of the trading strategies outlined above can be used for gap trading at the end of the day as well. You will need to use a stock scanner to determine the gapping stocks with the best potential for the best results. When you come across gapping stocks that are still increasing in volume then there is typically a good chance that the trend will continue. When a gapping stock crosses near the top of the resistance level this is often a reliable entry point. Likewise, a gapping short stock provides a viable entry point when the gap down crosses the support level.

Modified trading method: This trading method can be used with any of the gaps outlined above. The biggest difference with this method is that instead of waiting for the price of the given stock to break above the high or below the low you take an entry point that is in the midst of the rebound period. In order for this method to be successful you should only use it with stocks that have been trading at roughly twice their average volume for at least 5 days. Likewise, you need to ensure you have a fast trade execution system as stocks with heavy volume can reverse quite quickly. For this reason, mental stops, as opposed to hard stops, are recommended for the best results.

Gap and go: The gap and go strategy is an important one to master when it comes to chasing long-term success in the day trading arena. This strategy is specifically for use between 9:30 am and 10 am and is a great way to start the day with a few quick and easy trades. Many potential gap traders tend to focus on the gap between close of the previous day and today's open after things have settled down somewhat at the 10:30 am mark. The gap and go, on the other hand, focuses on taking advantage of the market forces that must be at work in order to generate differentials between close and open in the first place.

To utilize this strategy, you are going to want to determine which stocks have experienced either a gap up or a gap down between close and open. You will then want to go short or long depending, while placing stop losses slightly above or below the open as needed. You will then need to manage the position and trail the stop as needed to prevent loss. This strategy is useful first thing in the morning because you will receive practically instantaneous feedback regarding the effectiveness of your decision. If you are wrong you will know right away as your stop loss will trigger or, if you are right, you will definite positive movement on your position and possibly quite a bit of it.

In order to make the most of this strategy you will want to utilize some filters as well. As an example, a gap of just a few points is unlikely to be of much use, even if it moves in your preferred direction. On the other hand, a gap of 15 points or more has the potential to generate a realistic profit. Additionally, you are going to want to keep an eye out for gaps that form with substantial room between the next level of support or resistance as is relevant. If the gap is close to the level in question then it is unlikely to move much, however, if the distance is notable then the odds of profitable movement are even greater.

Trading these early morning gaps is a great way to take advantage of the path of least resistance. Even if they don't end up going anywhere useful on a given day they are quick and easy to set up, and always have the potential for significant profit. Just be sure to use accurate risk and trade management skills and there is no reason you shouldn't find success with them on a regular basis.

CHAPTER 3: REVERSAL DAY TRADING STRATEGY

A reversal occurs when the direction of an existing price trend rapidly changes directions abruptly to run parallel to the prevailing trend. On a price chart, reversals can be easily determined after they have hit the new point of resistance and dropped back the way they started. Reversals are also known as corrections, rallies or trend reversals.

An uptrend which is moving along with a series of higher lows and higher highs will reverse into a downtrend and start showing a series of lower lows and lower highs. The opposite can be said of an existing downtrend. Reversals typically occur most frequently in intraday trading as long timeframes tend to smooth things out overall. These types of reversals can happen as part of natural market correction but are more commonly seen as the result of news releases or other occurrences that suddenly change the evaluation of a given stock.

By keeping a close eye on technical indicators, successful traders can often determine when a reversal is occurring before it has fully formed. Additionally, if a stock has been reaching record highs or lows, then it is often natural to assume that a reversal is at hand. Specifically, you will find candlestick movements useful when it comes to determining these shifts as quickly as possible. While many traders content themselves with successfully calling bottoms or tops, the best reversal traders only enter the field once the top or bottom has already formed. Trading reversals successfully often means standing by as you wait for the perfect setup to unfold.

Mentally, it can be quite difficult to get into the reversal trading mindset because so many day traders are primed to make trades as quickly as possible when signals turn in their favor. Getting over this mental hump is key to successfully trading reversals in the long term.

In order to trade reversals successfully, it is important to never use pending orders when you know the price is approaching your target level. Additionally, you need to prepare yourself to miss out on a certain portion of the profits every time. This is an unavoidable part of the process and will ensure you win more than you lose in the long run. Finally, it is important to keep in mind that not every reversal is going to lead to an entry point. Watch your signals and don't be over anxious to chase a pattern that isn't actually materializing.

Basic reversal strategy

Find the right timeframe: The basis of all successful reversal trades involves taking a broad view of the day as a whole. This means the 4-hour or the daily charts. You will then want to add in the lines that really stand out or that were the origin of previous significant price movements.

Both resistance and support along with demand and supply level concepts can be useful when it comes to identify price levels that are especially high impact. It is important to keep in mind how important the right indicators are to the process as attempting reversals without them is little better than predicting standard market moves, which, in itself, is little better than simply gambling. Oftentimes this strategy will result in reversals that take place in mid-air, far away from your determined levels. These trades are going to have a low probability of success which means that trying to get into these reversals is not worth your time.

Choose the right reversal signal: Once the price has reached your desired level, it is important to be patient and then continue being patient as this step could take a while. Frequently you won't notice a clear signal at all and the price will start moving without you. This will happen and the sooner you learn to accept it the more effective of a reversal trader you will be. In fact, this is what your trading rules are for, they help you to filter out the price movements that are not going to be worth your time, leaving only those setups with the highest probabilities ready and waiting for you.

In general, the more pronounced time frame reversal signals are going to show themselves in the form of momentum divergences visible on either a MACD or RSI. They may also present themselves as a spike moving through an outer Bollinger band. A Fibonacci sequence that has been completed successfully will also show you are on the right track.

None of these are the true signal, however, so you will have to wait a little while longer before pulling the trigger. These signals tend to occur most frequently at the tops or the bottoms of the market and are then flooded by novice traders eager to jump on the emerging trend. Waiting until the reversal is already moving in your favor will always produce better results.

Look for the broken market structure: What you are waiting for is a lower timeframe entry trigger, which is without a doubt the hardest part of trading reversals successfully. While you would likely be able to turn a profit by entering earlier on certain trades, you are also more likely to lose out as well. Being patient is the best way to keep your overall win rate intact.

Once you see the right trend start to form, you are going to want to switch to a lower timeframe view. At the lower timeframe, you will then want to wait for the right entry point to be confirmed based on micro market structures. One of these is a new set of highs and lows. Alternately, you could also keep an eye out for resistance and support level breaks or breaks in the trendline to trigger your entry point.

Making the most from the trade: Once you are in the trade you are going to want to put all of your focus onto Bollinger bands. As long as the price keeps a reasonable distance from the outer bands then the reversal is still occurring to an acceptable degree. A singular spike in the middle of the Bollinger bands will not signal an exit either, this will only occur when a close violates the middle Bollinger band. In order to ensure your results are consistent, it is important to always make the same decisions based on the available data. For example, if you used the 1-hour chart to determine your entry point then you would want to use it again to determine the best time to exit.

3 bar reversal pattern

3 bar patterns are one of the most common successful trade setups. This is caused by the fact that they are simple for novice traders to set up after they have completed their scans. This is also

one of the reasons that the 3 bar reversal pattern can be difficult to use, simply because the setup can be found practically anywhere you look. In order to reduce the number of potential setups you can see in an intraday basis, you are going to want to add some extra requirements to the setup in order to filter out additional market noise.

Signals: First and foremost, you are only going to want to target stocks that are strongly trending in one direction. Second, the low (downtrend) or high (uptrend) bar needs to occur in the middle of a candlestick. Finally, the final bar needs to close either above the high of the first two candlesticks. With this standard in place it will then be painfully obvious once a given trend has reversed.

Unlike the preceding strategy, this strategy works in a variety of timeframes. As an example, assume you are working off of the 5-minute chart before detecting a stock that hit its low and then sharply reversed upwards. The third bar in the series would then close at a point that is higher than the highs of both of the other bars. While you can move forward if the close is above the high of the middle candlestick, it is better to know what the third candle is doing for added insurance.

The exit strategy for this pattern is just a simple moving average or even a price target. Just be sure you watch it closely and you should be fine. A good rule of thumb with this pattern is a 3 to 1 risk and reward ratio for the trade. Additionally, it is important to keep in mind that this strategy can generate quick returns no matter what time of day it is and in any market type.

False signals: These days, more and more day traders are trying to fake one another out when it comes to specific trades. Unfortunately, the 3 bar reversal pattern is not immune to this problem. One of the main reasons that the 3 bar reversal pattern fails is when volatility isn't high enough. If the market is exceedingly choppy, then the formation you are looking for is really going to be nothing more than a pause in the overall action.

This means it will not ultimately result in the type upswing or downswing that you are looking for. Adding in additional methods of confirmation before you choose your entry point will make it easier to avoid these false signals. If you buy into this type of trend it is important to be aware that it isn't moving as you would like and cut your losses before they get worse. The sooner you bail, the sooner you can get back to looking for a reversal that is actually profitable.

Hook reversal

A hook reversal is a candlestick pattern that materializes on the shorter timeframe charts. They can appear both on downtrends and uptrends and are useful when it comes to predicting a reversal in the current trend. This pattern appears as a candlestick with a higher low as well as a lower high when compared to the candlestick of the previous day. This is a somewhat unique pattern as the size difference between the body of the first and second bar is quite small when compared to other engulfing patterns.

When this pattern is found as part of an uptrend then the open will typically be near the previous high while the low will be near the previous low. This pattern is typically associated with other harami positions because the body of the second candle is formed inside the body of the first candle. As a signal for a reversal, this pattern's strength comes from the strength of the trend. The strong the trend, the stronger the signal given off by the pattern.

Abandoned baby

Bullish abandoned baby: This is another candlestick pattern that is useful when it comes to determining the potential for a reversal in the current trend. This pattern is formed by a trio of candlesticks with several distinctive characteristics. The first bar is going to be a red candlestick that is large and visible within a previously defined downtrend. The second bar will have an open equal to its close that gaps beneath the close of the first bar. The final bar is going to be a white candlestick that is large and opens higher than the second bar. This bar also represents changing trader sentiment.

This is a somewhat rare pattern but is reliable when it comes to predicting a change in the dominant downtrend. The accuracy of the signal is then further enhanced when combined with additional technical indicators including RSI and MACD.

Bearish abandoned baby: This candlestick pattern is useful when it comes to signaling a reversal in an existing uptrend. It is also a trio pattern and the first part is a white candlestick that is large and found within a previously defined uptrend. The second bar is the same as that found in the bullish abandoned baby. The final bar is a red candle that is large and will open beneath the second bar. It is also useful when it comes to determining current trader sentiment. As with the bullish abandoned baby, this is a rare but useful pattern. It signifies coming changes to the uptrend.

Outside reversal

This is a price chart pattern in which a stock's low and high prices for the day both exceed those of the previous trading session. This pattern is also known as a bearish engulfing pattern if the second bar is a down candlestick and a bullish engulfing pattern if the second bar is an up candlestick. This pattern is useful when it comes to identifying potential price movement and determining if it is likely to be bearish or bullish.

It occurs at the point a price bar falls outside the range of a previous price bar when its high is greater than the previous high and its low is lower than the previous low. As a general rule, if the outside reversal occurs at the level of resistance then the signal is bearish and if it occurs at the support level then it is bullish.

Three stars in the south

This is a bullish 3 candle pattern that indicates a reversal is on its way. It occurs when the market is currently in a downtrend. The first candle will be black with a longer than average real body, a longer than average lower shadow and no upper shadow to speak of. The second candle will also be black with a shorter real body and a low that is above the first candle's low. The final candle will also be black and include a short body with no shadows and a close that is in the hi-lo range of the middle candle.

The theory behind this pattern states that bears will always lose momentum over time which will eventually ensure the bulls rally and reverse the existing trend. While extremely accurate when it comes to predicting reversals, it very rarely materializes on the charts. The reversals it predicts are also typically mild which means the upside will be small for those traders who bet on the decline. It is most useful as a signal to exit a currently held short position or initiate a long position for a small profit.

Buy weakness

This is a trading strategy that takes a proactive approach when it comes to closing out a short position or buying into a new long position. This is a useful strategy when the price of a given stock is currently falling but is expected to reverse quickly. The opposite of this strategy is useful when it comes to prices that are currently rising which is known as selling into strength.

As an example, consider a stock that is likely going to fall from $5 to $4.50 before then rising to a new point that is above $5. You would then buy into the stock as it was weakening at a price point lower than $5 and then wait until the trend reverses. You would then hold it long enough for the price to move above $5 in order to turn a profit. If you were a short seller you could also buy into the weakness by simply closing out your position. This would involve purchasing the falling stock in the anticipation that the price will soon change direction and begin to rise.

It is common for many traders to wait for a confirmation of the impending change before reacting to a new trend. This strategy allows you to get in as early as possible in order to maximize your profits from the eventual movement. This strategy provides you with greater room for error but should only be utilized if you have utter confidence that the reversal is coming as otherwise it has too great of a chance to cost you money.

Risk reversal

This is a hedging strategy that involves selling a call and buying a put option. This then mitigates the risk of downward price movements that are unfavorable while limiting the total potential for profit from any upward movements that occur. If you are trading in the forex market then the risk reversal is the difference in volatility between the put and the call.

If you are short on an underlying instrument then hedging with this position involves implementing a long risk reversal via the purchase of a call option. You would then write a put option on the same underlying asset. On the other hand, if you are long on an underlying asset then you would short the risk reversal to hedge the position via the writing of a call and the purchasing of a put option related to the same underlying asset.

CHAPTER 4: WEDGE STRATEGY

Falling and rising wedges are a type of technical chart pattern that is useful when it comes to predicting both trend reversals as well as trend continuations. They form naturally on the chart as the market trends in a specific direction. Wedges are also known to appear near the end of both bearish and bullish trends. As such, wedges can have either reversal or continuation characteristics depending both on the direction of the trend as well as the type of wedge that forms.

Rising wedges: Rising wedge chart patterns typically develop when the price is hitting very high tops and extremely high bottoms. The bottoms tend to increase faster than the tops. This then causes the wedge to form an ascending corridor with the walls narrowing until the lines connect at an apex point. This formation really only signifies the potential for a bearish move in the future. Depending on the direction the market is currently moving in, this could be seen as either the continuation of an existing trend or the start of a reversal. Regardless, if the price is in the midst of a rising wedge then the price will likely soon break through the lower level of the figure.

The rising wedge is often considered one of the most difficult chart patterns to recognize and trade accurately. Despite the fact that it is a consolidation formation, the lack of upside momentum from each reoccurring high point provides the pattern with a bearish feel. Yet, the series of high highs and moderate lows keep it firmly in the bullish category. The final break of support will indicate the forces of supply typically win out which means the price is likely to drop. There are no truly reliable ways to determine how much of a decline to expect, so using additional technical indicators is recommended.

In order for a rising wedge to qualify as a reversal pattern, there needs to be an existing pattern for it to reverse. Sometimes the entire trend will be contained within the rising wedge and they can continue for as long as 6 months. If you find a rising wedge pattern in the short term, take a look at the long-term charts and see if what you are seeing is actually a continuation of something much larger to ensure you make the right choices.

Falling wedge: A falling wedge looks like the inverse of a rising wedge. It forms when the price is experiencing significantly lower than average highs and lower than normal lows. The tops are going to decrease at a rate that is greater than the lows. Falling wedges indicate a movement towards bullishness in the market which can either be a continuation of the trend or a reversal. Regardless, the price is likely to break through the upper line of the formation at some point soon.

Sideways wedge: A sideways wedge forms when a range that is already moving sideways begins to narrow. It contains higher lows and lower highs and its trigger line is always practically flat with very little slope to speak of. This type of wedge is a good indicator that you are going to want to buy when prices are low, sell when they are high and avoid the middle all together. It also lets you know that you will have an equal opportunity for success with both as the market currently lacks a directional bias.

This wedge tells you that the market is currently in a state of confusion and that other investors lack the confidence to go all in one way or the other. This should also let you know to expect fake breakouts as the wedge indicates a lack of a firm direction which will be born out in the overall movement the breakout experiences. As long as you stick to the basics, this type of wedge says the market is yours for the taking.

Putting wedges to work

When it comes to determining the likely breakout direction for a falling or rising wedge, it can be quite confusing as they can easily go in either direction. The way to accurately determine the answer lies in accurately interpreting the events that lead up to wedge's creation.

Trend continuation: If the trend is likely to continue in its current direction then the wedge is likely to play the role of a pattern correction on the chart you are watching. As an example, assume you are tracking a bullish trend that suddenly develops a falling wedge. In this case it can be thought of as a correction which means you would expect the price to breakout from the upside of the wedge.

The same can be said for rising wedges. The biggest difference is that a rising wedge instead of a falling wedge would appear. Ultimately the direction of the break is determined by the price action. If a pair of rising wedges develop after a price increase has just occurred, then they likely represent the exhaustion of any previous bullish movement. After a pair of increases the tops of both will often look like a trend slowdown.

If a downtrend is occurring then the price is likely to increase after a falling wedge forms which means the price will decrease if a rising wedge forms. With this being the case, the rising wedge implies the continuation of a trend while the falling wedge indicates a reversal of the trend. While the roles of the pair of wedges can change, their potential and their behavior remains constant.

Resistance lines: For the upper resistance line, it takes at least 2 reaction highs to generate it properly, though 3 is even better. Each high should always be higher than the previous high for rising wedges and lower for falling wedges. The lower support line will also require two reaction lows, that are higher than the previous lows for rising wedges and lower for falling wedges. The upper and lower resistance points then converge as the pattern matures. The advances from the lows will become lower and lower for rising wedges and larger and larger for falling wedges. This will make any seeming rallies that occur increasingly unconvincing. If this occurs then the upper resistance line is likely to be unable to keep up with the lower support line which means a supply overhang is likely to form. This will lead to an increase in price.

Trend reversal: In some cases, a wedge will signal the reversal of a current pattern. In order to identify the reversal of a trend you will want to look for trends that are experiencing a slowdown of their main trend. This slowdown will typically terminate in a new wedge pattern. In these cases, it is common for both wedges to have the characteristics of a reversal. This is caused because the trend direction formations are opposites which means their moves are almost finished.

Trading falling and rising wedges

Entering the market: When it comes to entering the market, the first thing you will need to keep in mind is that each and every wedge uses a signal line. Depending on the type of wedge in question, this signal line will be either the upper (falling) or lower (rising) line of the pattern.

As an example, if you find a rising wedge then the signal line will be on the lower level that connects the bottoms of each point of the wedge. If you are dealing with a falling wedge then the line of the signal will connect the upper tops of the formation.

When you find a break in this single line then you will want to enter the market in the same direction as the break. As an example, if you are using a rising wedge then you will find the price of the stock breaking through the wedge's lover level which means you are going to want to go short. Likewise, when you see a falling wedge you will want to enter the market at the point the price breaks through the upper side of the wedge formation.

Use the correct timeframe: While occasionally the 1-hour chart can be used to accurately show the best wedges, the 4-hour and daily timeframe charts are often going to be your best bet. By staying away from the shorter timeframes, you will find that you have to deal with less intraday market noise. Additionally, you will find significantly fewer false breaks when compared to the 5 and 15-minute charts.

You may also find the greater timeframes give you more freedom overall which will translate into less frustration and anxiety which will make it easier for you to both find favorable trades and place them accurately. All together this will lead to a much smoother trading environment. As the mental aspect of day trading is 90 percent of finding success, this reduction of stress can be a real game changer.

Have realistic expectations: When it comes to trading wedges, it can be easy to overtrade, especially if you are using an extended time frame such as 4-hour or daily charts. Wedge trading is all about quality over quantity which means that you should be able to find success trading as few as 10 trades per month. Waiting for the right wedge setup to come along takes patience and if you get too anxious you will do little except hurt your overall trading percentage and cost yourself money. Instead of focusing on trading this strategy every day, focus on finding the right trades with the right risk and reward ratio to make it worth your time.

Placing a stop loss: When trading based on wedges the stop loss orders you place will need to be directly above the rising wedge or directly beneath the falling wedge. It is important that you do not place them too tightly as the action of the price movement will often violate one of the trendlines if you do. The price will then rebound swiftly but the damage will be done. You will instead want to look for a significant break in order to determine the right point to exit.

Taking profits: When it comes to determining the price target of this type of trade it is going to be equal to the wedge's size. As such, if you have a rising wedge then you can realistically expect the market to drop an amount that is equal to the size of the formation. If you see a falling wedge then the equity is likely to increase based on the size of the formation. If the trend is bullish then the price is likely to bounce from the trend. The price is also likely to start hesitating and close the rising wedge.

If the wedge is broken then the price is likely to decrease into a falling wedge. If the price touches the trend and the wedge breaks then the trend is likely going to move in a bullish direct.

CONCLUSION

Thank you for making it through to the end of *Day Trading: Strategies on How to Excel at Day Trading*, let's hope it was informative and able to provide you with all of the tools you need to achieve your day trading goals, whatever it is that they may be. Just because you've finished this book doesn't mean there is nothing left to learn on the topic, expanding your horizons is the only way to find the mastery you seek. Trading in the stock market can be a cutthroat experience and nowhere is it more cutthroat than in the world of day trading. As such, it is especially important to you continue to learn all you can and develop a ravenous need for new strategies because you can be sure that that is what your competition is doing.

Just because you are day trading, however, doesn't mean that you need to focus on constantly trading all of the time. The fact of the matter is that some days, and even some weeks, the market simply isn't going to want to cooperate. Truly successful traders learn to make the most of the good trades that come their way and not to force it on the days that absolutely nothing is happening. Forcing a trade where none exists is only going to cause you anxiety, frustration, cost you capital for trade fees and hurt your trade percentage to boot. Take advantage of the time off to clear your head and come back ready for success when the market is more agreeable. Focus on quality over quantity and you are far more likely to find the success you seek. Remember, day trading successfully is a marathon, not a sprint, slow and steady wins the race.

OPTIONS TRADING: STRATEGIES ON HOW TO EXCEL AT OPTIONS TRADING

DESCRIPTION

When it comes to having a little wiggle room in the stock market, options trading can't be beaten. The simple ability to choose whether or not you want to purchase the underlying stock attached to your options can easily lead to success in scenarios that would only lead to failure in the stock market. With that being said, however, in order to maximize your options trading experience, you need to be able to rely on successful strategies you can count on when the going gets tough. If you are looking to take your options trading game to the next level, then *Options Trading: Strategies on How to Excel at Options Trading* is the book that you have been waiting for.

Inside you will find over a dozen different strategies that can be used regardless of the market conditions or if you are selling or buying, and often both at once. You will find strategies that cover multiple types of spreads, notes for trading indices, the weekly options market, how to minimize an existing bad trade via the stock repair strategy and more.

Without a doubt, this book contains everything you need in order to stop questioning potential trades and start acting in a manner that will ensure you maximize your profits with every trade. After all, time is always of the essence when it comes to making the best trades and *Options Trading: Strategies on How to Excel at Options Trading* will get you to the place you need to be to stop second-guessing and start succeeding. No matter what level of risk you prefer or how long you have been in the options market, you will find something useful inside.

So, what are you waiting for? The options market is all about choice and now is the time to choose to stop wasting time on trades that do little more than break even. Take control of your trade experience and buy this book today!

Inside you will find

- The best time to utilize the index straddle and why you may want to consider options trading in the indices in general.

- The best way to break even on stocks that have already dropped out of the money.

- Spreads, spreads and more spreads. Nearly ten different spread strategies to ensure you have the right spread for every occasion.

- The top technical indicators for the options market that you likely aren't already using.

- The complete details on the little-known options trading market that is perfect for short term trades.

- All about combination strategies and why you need to start using them right now.

- *And more...*

INTRODUCTION

Congratulations on downloading *Options Trading: Strategies on How to Excel at Options Trading* and thank you for doing so. When it comes to having a little wiggle room in the stock market, options trading can't be beaten. The simple ability to choose whether or not you want to purchase the underlying stock attached to your options can easily lead to success in scenarios that would only lead to failure in the stock market. With that being said, however, in order to maximize your options trading experience, you need to be able to rely on successful strategies you can count on when the going gets tough.

To that end, the following chapters will discuss a wide variety of different options trading strategies designed to ensure that your time spent trading options is as fruitful and painless as possible. First, you will learn all about long and short combinations as well as when the best time to use each really is. Next, you will learn how to put straddles to use in the index market as well as the benefits of trading options in the index market in general. From there you will learn how to minimize the impact of a bad stock trade via the stock repair strategy.

Then you will learn how to use both vertical and horizontal spread strategies before learning all the details of ratio and front spread strategies as well. The talk of spread strategies then wraps up with a detailed discussion of both put and call backspread strategies. Up next you will learn about many of the technical indicators that work best with options trading and why you will always want to use multiple indicators no matter what. Finally, things will wrap up with a discussion of the pros and cons of weekly options trading and why it may be the right choice for you.

There are plenty of books on this subject on the market, thanks again for choosing this one! Every effort was made to ensure it is full of as much useful information as possible, please enjoy!

CHAPTER 1: COMBINATION STRATEGIES

Long combination

Also known as the synthetic long stock strategy, the long combination is utilized by purchasing a call and a put with the same details at the same strike price. You will want the underlying asset price to be quite close to the strike price when you pull the trigger. This is a bullish strategy, and the short put is uncovered which leaves you with a significant amount of risk if things go wrong. As such, this strategy is only recommended when the indicators you favor show that the market is likely to move in the way you expect.

This strategy is known as the synthetic long stock due to the fact that the risk and reward are nearly the same as the more common long stock strategy. Additionally, if you hold onto the position until it expires you will likely end up purchasing the underlying asset anyway. Specifically, if the underlying asset ends up higher than the strike price, then you will want to exercise the call. Meanwhile, if it is below the strike price, it is very likely that the put will be assigned which means you will still need to purchase the asset.

With that being said, there is no limit to how much you want the underlying asset to move once you have set up this strategy, the more positive momentum it has, the more money you stand to make. The maximum amount you can expect to lose if things don't go according to plan is limited to the amount of the strike price plus the net debit or minus the net credit.

In this case, purchasing the call will give you the right to purchase the underlying asset at the strike price. Selling the put at the same price then obligates you to purchase the underlying asset at this price if you find yourself in a situation where the option is assigned.

Time decay is a relatively neutral factor for this strategy. On the other hand, it will erode the value of the purchased option which is far from ideal. On the other hand, it will also decrease the value of the option being sold. Likewise, the implied volatility of this option is fairly neutral as well. It will increase the value of the option being sold while doing the same to the option being purchased.

While on paper this strategy might not seem more beneficial than simply purchasing the underlying asset directly, the fact of the matter is that the leverage in play makes it worthwhile to purchase the option instead. Specifically, this way you get all of the same benefits as purchasing directly while still allowing your money to work for you in other capacities until the option expires.

Furthermore, when you first start this strategy, you will have additional requirements when it comes to margin due to the short put. You will also need to pay a net debit in order to establish the position. These costs will still be relatively small compared to the upfront price of the underlying asset.

When utilizing this strategy, it is important to be aware that the price of the underlying asset is rarely going to sit precisely at the strike price. If this price is above the strike price, then the call will typically cost more than the put which means you will start with a greater net debit. The opposite is also true and will result in a net credit.

Carry costs and dividends will also come into play with this strategy. As an example, if a company that previously never paid dividends suddenly started up this practice then the prices of both calls and puts are sure to change. This will occur due to the fact that the underlying stock price will be expected to drop by the amount of the dividend right after the dividend is paid. This, in turn, will cause the price of puts to increase and the price of calls to decrease before the stock price drops due to the anticipation of the decrease. As such, if the put cost exceeds the call cost then you will be able to use this strategy with a net credit.

Short combination

Also known as the synthetic short stock, this strategy is put into effect by purchasing a put and a call at the same strike price with the same characteristics. The best time to pursue this strategy is when the underlying asset is close to the strike price. As with the long combination, this strategy has the potential for great risk. However, also like the long combination there is no limit to how much you want the underlying asset to move as the further down it goes the greater your opportunity for profit is going to be.

The amount you can expect to make on the strategy is determined by the amount the underlying asset moves from the strike price minus any debits or adding any credits that were generated during its creation. If you hold onto the position until it reaches the point of expiration you are almost always going to end up selling either because the call has been assigned or because it is a good value.

In this instance, both time decay and implied volatility are going to remain mostly neutral. This is the case because it affects both sides of the strategy in equal amounts.

When starting this strategy, you are going to receive a net credit most of the time, but there will also be some margin requirements due to the short call. These costs are going to be relatively small when compared to the amount that you could make the trade, however. One of the number one reasons this strategy is used is that it doesn't require much cash to be held up via margin when creating the short stock position.

It is also important to keep in mind potential changes to the price based on dividends as they will determine if this strategy can be established for a net debit or a net credit. However, this is a useful strategy if you own a particular stock that you plan on shorting and that stock has a pending dividend. Typically, if you are short stock, then you will have to pay the dividends from your own account, but if you use this strategy, that requirement will not apply.

CHAPTER 2: INDEX STRADDLES

Purchasing an index straddle requires you to buy an index put and an index call from the same index, with the same strike price and expiration month. A long straddle position is frequently obtained and then sold at the same time in an effort to generate a larger profit or minimize loss. In this strategy, as long as you hold both the put as well as the call then your investment is hedged. This is due to the fact that the call has the potential to increase in value as the index rises and the put have the potential to increase in value as the value of the index decreases.

Purchasing an index straddle provides you with the benefits of both the index call and the index put. It also leverages the profit potential when the underlying index moves significantly in either direction from the entry point. Alternately, those who purchase straddles may instead focus on short-term gains when the volatility levels change despite a lack of significant movement from the related index. This typically leads to smaller, more reliable profits. Regardless of the path you choose, the amount of risk you run will be both predetermined and limited.

You should consider purchasing an index straddle if you are fairly confident the index is going to move in a big way, but you don't know if that move will be up or down. It is also a fine choice if you expect the volatility of the index to increase both up and down near the current level while at the same time expecting an increase in the implied volatility of the overlying options. Finally, it is ideal if you prefer a limited amount of risk but would still prefer to utilize the added leverage that options provide.

As with any long index trade, the options holder always has the opportunity to exercise the option prior to, or at the point of, its expiration. Additionally, the option can be sold in the marketplace as they almost always retain their market value throughout a greater portion of the time prior to their expiration.

This strategy is not especially bearish or bullish but instead is a combination of the two. The potential for profit of the long call at the point of expiration can be quite large as long as the underlying index continues to increase past the initial breakeven point. Likewise, the long put has the same potential assuming the related index continues to decrease steadily from the starting point. The long index straddle is only limited by the momentum of the movement, not the movement itself.

This strategy has two separation breakeven points for when the options expire. The upside breakeven point is equal to the contract of the underlying index level's strike price plus any premiums paid for the put and the call. The downside breakeven point is the index level that is equal to the strike price minus the cost of the call and the premium on the put.

Volatility increases are positive for this strategy while lowered volatility has a negative effect that is more prevalent that either the basic put or long call due to the dual nature of the strategy. Regardless, time decay will always have a negative effect on this strategy.

Index   straddle   example
A good example of the right time to utilize an index straddle is as follows. For the sake of this example assume the Federal Reserve has let it be known that it is considering raising the Fed Funds rate in an effort to combat inflation.

This decision will go into effect next month and was influenced primarily by producer and consumer price data that will be made available to the public in the interim. An increase in the interest rate would likely cause index prices to decrease sharply. Maintaining the status quo may boost them to record highs. All told the market is likely to move in one direction or the other by 5 percent or more in the month following the announcement.

With this information in hand, let's say that you are interested in a specific index that is currently sitting at 100. You would then purchase a one-month call (assume the current cost is $1.70) and a put (assume the rate is $1.50). The total cost for the index straddle strategy is then $3.20 multiplied by 100 for a total of $320. By making this purchase, you are indicating that you anticipate the index is going to move beyond one of the breakeven points.

In this scenario, the upside breakeven point would be $3.20 plus the 100 strike price for a total of $103.20. The downside breakeven point would be 100-$3.20 for a total of $96.80. The potential for profit in this situation is essentially unlimited assuming the price of the index increases to a point above 103.20 or drops below 96.80 before the expiration date. The risk for this strategy is set at the premium of $320 and would only come into play if the price of the index doesn't move at all, staying at 100 for the entire month.

If the price moves in enough of a positive or negative direction, then you would be free to sell both the call and the put in the open marketplace to take advantage of the gain. However, if things don't change enough to realize the profit, then it is likely that you would have to sell at a loss thanks to the effect of time decay.

If the index ends up closes at a point above the 103.2 breakeven point (at 105 for this example), then the put is going to expire out of the money and end up being worthless. The call will be on the money, however, which means it will be worth its intrinsic value which can be determined by the difference between the index level and its strike price. In this case, it would be $105-$100 for a gain of $5 per share or $500 in this scenario. The same would be true if the put expires in the money and the call expires worthlessly. The total profit is then tallied by subtracting $3.20 from $5 for a profit of $1.80 or 180 on 100 shares.

The biggest risk in this instance is if the index doesn't change at all, leaving the price at $100 and ensuring a total loss of the initial $320 investment. Meanwhile, if the index moved upwards to 102, then the put would expire worthlessly and out of the money while the call would have an intrinsic value of $2 per share which, while still a positive amount, is not enough movement to actually turn a profit. The best course of action in this scenario would still be to sell, however, as you will be able to recoup more than half of your losses.

Instead of being motivated purely by the potential price movement, you could instead be motivated by how much you expect the volatility of a given index to change over the predetermined period. In this case, assume that at the start of the 30 days the index had a volatility level of 14 percent and after 10 days it has already increased to 19 percent. With this information, you can then determine what the likely amount of profit is going to be at the end of the 30 days.

You can then expect the call to be at an expected value of $1.85 (up from $1.70) and the put to have an expected value of $1.70 (up from $1.50). This would then indicate that the expected value at the end of the 30 days would be about $3.50 which is enough to turn a $30 profit when it expires. While not great, it is practically guaranteed which means that it can be used to offset extra costs associated with riskier trades. This $30 then represent a return of 9.4 percent in just 10 days.

When you hold onto an index straddle for the purpose of waiting for an anticipated volatility increase, you are in a sense protected from large movements that may happen suddenly. In fact, if the index level ends up moving dramatically while you are on the hook for the index sample you can even make a profit on the value of the put or the call without any increase in the implied volatility.

CHAPTER 3: STOCK REPAIR STRATEGY

This is a great strategy to employ if you have already purchased shares of stock that are optionable and are stuck in a situation where you are watching its value decline with no clear recourse to rectify the situation. If the stock you purchased was non-actionable, then all you would be able to do is hold onto it in hopes that things turn around or double down in hopes of turning a profit at a lower breakeven point. Luckily, with optionable stocks, you also have a third alternative.

The stock repair strategy is ideal for those who are looking to break even on a stock that they purchased at a point significantly higher than where the current market price stands and are looking to break even. It is important to keep in mind that you will need to be willing to forfeit any profit potential, even at the reduced breakeven point. This is also a good choice if you can't or are unwilling to commit any additional funds to the position in question.

The repair strategy is useful in helping you break even, especially if you are already in losing position. To utilize it you are going to want to sell 2 call options at a strike price above the current stock price and purchase 1 call option at the current price for every 100 shares of the failing stock you own. All of the options should have the same period of expiration. These sales and purchases are constructed in such a way that the additional funds you have to invest are slim to none.

Stock repair example

As an example, consider that you started out with 100 shares of a stock that you purchased for $50 a piece only to watch them fall to the current price of $40 each. You are unwilling to invest anything else into this stock and are afraid to take any more downside risk. Once you are ready simply to break even, then it is time to initiate the stock repair strategy.

To begin, you would want to purchase a single 60-day call option on the stock at the $40 price point for $3 while also selling 2 60-day call options at $1.50. It is important to keep in mind that the spread won't cost you any credits or debits. This is because the cost of the calls you purchased at the rate of $3 per 100 shares for a total of $300, will be completely offset by the premium that is generated from the sale of the written calls at the rate of $1.50x2x100 for a total of $300.

The purchase of the $40 call will provide you with the opportunity to purchase another 100 shares at the $40 price point while the 2 $45 calls will mean that you have to sell 200 shares at $45 if you are assigned. While you currently only have 100 shares, you could exercise the $40 long call to generate the required extra shares and make $5 per share at a relative profit of $500 which would cover the assignment.

There are several different likely scenarios that will come into play at the point the options expire. First, the underlying stock could continue to decrease and close around $35. It could remain at the current rate and close at $40. It could also regain some lost ground and close at $45. The best-case scenario is that it rises back to the price purchase price of $50 per share.

If the underlying stock continues to decrease in value and ends at $35, then all 3 of the calls will expire worthlessly out of the money. As the option position didn't cost anything to execute you wouldn't be out any more money that you would if you had simply held the stock and waited to see what would happen. As such the strategy has no negative or positive effect. This illustrates a salient point that this strategy will do nothing to protect you from additional losses to the underlying stocks. As such, if you expect the price to continue to fall after the initial decrease then a different strategy is recommended.

If the underlying stock remains at the $40 price point until the options expire then all of the call options will expire without any value. Once again, nothing extra was lost in the construction of the strategy, and you would be in the same position from where you started. If nothing else has changed, setting up a new round of calls and attempting the strategy again is recommended.

If the underlying stock rises in value to the point that is only $5 less than when you first purchased it then the short calls at the $45 price point will expire without value. However, the long call can then be sold at a $5 profit per share as the strategy was implemented with no additional costs. This, in turn, will reduce the amount lost on the original price decline to just $5 per share instead of $10 per share. After the $5 profit is factored in you will actually break even via this occurrence. Essentially what is managed in this scenario is that you have lowered the initial breakeven point from $50 to

$45, breaking even without requiring the underlying stock to recover past the original purchase price.

If the price of the underlying stock rallies back to the original price of $50 per share then the long shares will be in a breakeven position, the long call at $40 will be worth $10, and the short calls will now be worth -$5 each. The net result of this will be that you still breakeven overall with the gains and the losses canceling one another out. Even if the price continues to rise past the $50 point, you will still be unable to make a profit as the mixture of calls will continue to cancel one another out.

As such, if you feel as though there is a chance that the underlying stock is going to rally, then in order to mitigate the constant breakeven status you would want to liquidate the new positions you created as quickly as possible. You could sell the $40 call for the intrinsic value it holds of $10 and purchase the $45 calls for their intrinsic value of $5 and close out the strategy for just the added commission costs. With this done you would then be left free and clear on your 100 shares and once again able to profit from prices increases past the original $50.

Determine the right strike price

One of the most important considerations that come along with establishing a repair strategy that can be as effective as possible is determining the right option to purchase and the correct one to sell. The $5 price chosen in the above example took half of the unrealized loss into account. As such, if you started with an underlying stock priced at $100 and were currently sitting with shares at $90 then you would want to purchase calls at $90 and sell calls at

amazon.com

order of December 11, 2017 (Order ID 111-1 74229-847863?)

Item	Item Price	Total
Miger (3Pack) Apple Certified 6.5Ft 2 in 1 Lightning and Micro USB Cable Nylon Braided Sync and Charging Cable Cord for ... Wireless Phone Accessory X001LGQ6ER MO-6ZVH-C073 770659646055 (Sold by yangshichen g666)	$14.66	$14.66

Shipment completes your order.

	Subtotal	$14.66
feedback on how we packaged	Order Total	$14.66
order.? Tell us at www.amazon.com/	Paid via credit/debit	$14.66
aging.		

rn or replace your item
Amazon.com/returns

2dymndr9/-2 of 2-/-/-GT-COMCA-S/second/9152768/1212-22:30/1212-15.13

V3

$100 as $10 is half the unrealized loss. If you plan on purchasing at the money options, then you will want to sell out of the money options that are halfway between the current price of the underlying stock and the price you originally paid.

Furthermore, it is important to keep in mind that the repair strategy will not work successfully for every stock that is currently trading below the purchase price. The strategy tends to be effective for stocks that are down up to 20 percent from their original purchase point as long as options are utilized with a range of between 60 and 90 days. However, it is ineffective if the underlying stock has already dropped as much as 40 or 50 percent. In these cases, the selling of a pair of out of the money calls will not make up the difference and generate a large enough premium to balance out the cost of the single at the money call.

Finally, it is important to keep in mind that the stock repair strategy can often be initiated for a small debit or credit. You may still want to consider it a viable strategy if you have to pay up to $.50 for initiating the position. If this is the case, then you will need to give up a small debit regardless of how high the underlying stock will ultimately increase in price. However, the effectiveness of the strategy may still outweigh these additional costs.

On the other hand, however, if the option position is established for a credit that is slightly above the break-even point then you might keep the credit. The final loss or profit scenarios use this strategy will then vary depending on the original price of the underlying stock when it was purchased, the price of the stock when the repair strategy was put into play, whether a debit or credit was required to establish the position and the strike prices chosen.

CHAPTER 4: VERTICAL AND HORIZONTAL SPREAD STRATEGIES

Spread options trading strategies are useful in a wide variety of market conditions including bearish, neutral and bullish. Essentially, they function by limiting risk at the cost of limiting profits as well. Spread trading is defined as opening a position by selling and buying multiples of either puts or calls at the same time. If you buy a put or a call while also selling another put or a call with many of the same defining characteristics, then you can consider yourself a spread trader.

This strategy limits risk as you will always know the difference between the strike prices or the expiration dates of the given options. This difference is often referred to as the spread which gives this type of strategy its name.

Vertical spread

A vertical spread is a type of spread option where the 2 options you purchased, one to sell and one to buy, have the same expiration date and a different strike price. As an example, if you purchase one $60 option for stock A and sell a $70 option for stock A then you will have generated a vertical spread. To understand the benefits of this strategy, consider the following example.

Assume you own an underlying stock that is currently valued at $50 which you expect to rise a modest amount to $55. In order to take advantage of this opportunity, you are going to want to start a vertical spread. To do so, you purchase a $50 call option while at the same time selling a call option for $55. The $50 call is in the money which means it has a $1 premium while the $55 call has a $.25 premium as it is $5 out of the money. You would then pay $1 for the $50 call and earn $.25 on the $55 call, so the entire strategy costs you $.75 to set up.

From this point, one of two things can happen. The stock can either increase in price as you assumed it would, or it can drop below the current price and take you by surprise. Assume that you made a poor prediction and the price dropped from $50 to $45. Both the calls will then expire out of the money, and you don't need to do anything but close the position out of the money. The loss in this instance would be just $.75.

On the contrary, if the price did what you expected and rose to $55 then the $50 call would now be in the money for $5 which means it has a premium of $6. The $55 call is also now in the money and will also have a premium of $1. You cannot simply wait until the option expires in this scenario because the call you sold is now a naked call which is a call that is not currently covered by stocks you own. As such, you will need to close your position before the options expire to protect your position.

This means you will need to sell the $50 call for a profit while buying back the $55 call that was sold earlier. You would then want to sell the call for $6 and purchase the other call for $1. This transaction will then have earned you $4.25 total net gain once the $1 profit and the cost of the transaction have both been taken into account.

While this is all well and good, if, instead, the price jumps to $60 instead of $66 then the limited profit side of the equation comes in along with the limited risk. If the current price is $60, then the $50 call would be in the money to $10 which means it has an $11 premium. The $55 call would then be on the money as well and have a $6 premium. If you choose to close this position out at this time, then you would still make $5 overall, and $4.25 after fees are taken into account.

Once both of the calls have made it to in the money status, then the total profit is always going to be limited by the difference of the pair of strike prices after all the fees have been taken into account. In general, after the value of the underlying stock reaches the lower call you will start to earn a profit. Once it reaches past the higher call, then the maximum amount of profit has been reached.

Regardless of the fact that the potential for profit is limited, the fact that it costs less to execute than a traditional call option makes it worthwhile in cases where you do not believe the price of the underlying stock is going to move very much. This strategy is ideal for stocks that are currently experiencing a period of moderate bullishness.

Horizontal Spread

Also known as time spreads or calendar spreads, horizontal spreads are a type of spread where the strike price of the pair of options stays the same but the time in which they expire is different. All options have a time value associated with their costs. As time goes by, an option's premium typically begins to lose value based on the amount of time it has left as it is less likely to turn a profit in the shorter remaining time period. Additionally, the closer the expiration date looms the greater the decrease in value that can be expected. The horizontal spread uses the premium decay to your advantage.

As an example, assume that you are currently in the middle of the month of June when you decide to use a horizontal spread on an underlying stock. Assume the strike price of an option expiring in August is $4 while the strike price of the option that expires in September is $4.50.

To initiate this spread, you would want to sell the August option as it is the nearer of the two and then buy the option that is farther out (September in this case). As such you would earn $4 on the sale of the first option and then spend $4.50 when purchasing the second which means it would cost you $.50 overall to set up this trade.

Assume you then hold onto the options until the middle of August, and the option with the August expiration date is fast approaching. At this point in time, the premium on it has dropped substantially so now it only costs $1.50. At this point, the September option still has a month's room to move about, so the premium is holding firm at $3. At this point, you would want to close the spread position. You would purchase the August option back for $1.50 and sell the September option for $3, thus generating a $1.50 profit. Once you subtract the initial $.50 you still have a $1 profit. This technique is as effective for calls as it is for puts.

Chapter 5: Ratio Spread Strategy

The ratio spread trading strategy is a variation of the vertical spread strategy which involves an option spread using the same expiration date for multiple strategies. This is a neutral strategy that is useful when it comes to taking advantage of an underlying stock that has an extremely low amount of volatility. Much as the name implies, this strategy works by setting up an opening at a ratio of options sold to the number of options bought. The specific ratio can vary based on your personal needs, though the examples outlined below will deal with a 2 to 1 ratio of options sold to options bought.

Ratio spread strategies are an ideal companion when it comes to stocks that are certified non-volatile. Broadly, they are similar to trading strategies such as the butterfly or the iron condor with one major difference. Specifically, ratio spreads have a greater chance of loss if the underlying stock ends up being too volatile. This risk is then offset due to the fact that these spreads are built using fewer options total which means there will be fewer commission costs related to opening and closing the positions.

Put ratio spread

The put ratio spread has a neutral risk and profit profile that is constructed, unsurprisingly, by using put options. To put it into play you are going to want to purchase one put option that is in the money and sell two more put options that are current for the money. This strategy can be put into play for practically no upfront cost and may actually end up generating a small amount of profit. This occurs because the cost of the in the money option is going to be very close to, or less than, the amount made when selling the two at the money options.

It is important to keep in mind that the put ratio spread will not generate extra losses or profit if the underlying stock price rises above the in the money price of the first put options strike price. This is the case because if this occurs then all of the put options will expire worthlessly. After the price of the underlying stock dips below the in the money strike price, you will be able to earn a profit by selling the in the money option that was previously purchased. This profit will continue to increase as the price of the underlying stock continues to dip.

However, it is also important to keep in mind that once the price of the underlying stock drops below the at the money strike price of the puts you are selling the potential for profit will start to decrease rapidly. At this point, the at the money put options will no longer expire as worthless and must be bought back to prevent additional losses. As this will require you to purchase 2 options while only selling 1 the losses will continue to mount as the price of the underlying stock continues to drop.

As such, the put ratio spread can be thought to have a profit profile that is neutral with a slightly bullish tinge. It can achieve maximum profit only if the underlying stock price ends at the at the money put strike price. When this occurs, you can then sell the in the money put option while letting the other pair expire. Upward volatility will not generate additional profits or losses as all three puts will be affected equally and cancel out the greater profits. Meanwhile, losses due to downward volatility are going to be practically limitless. As such, this strategy should only be used with stocks that are neutral and non-volatile, and you are confident that they will stay this way until the strategy is complete.

Call ratio spread

The call ratio spread strategy uses call options in a variation of the standard vertical spread that uses a ratio of call options, most commonly in a 2:1 format. This is a neutral strategy that is best used on stocks that show a low degree of volatility. To utilize this strategy, you are going to want to purchase one in the money call option while selling a pair of call options that are at the money. As you are selling a greater number of options than you are purchasing, it is important to keep in mind that the additional options are going to be uncovered which makes the potential for loss significant if you choose poorly.

Due to this fact, the call ratio spread is considered a neutral strategy that is only suitable for non-volatile stocks. It creates a scenario where a falling stock price generates little to no losses while gains create the potential for unlimited losses. Be careful when using them and ensure that there are no news releases forthcoming as this can easily change a low-volatility stock into one with a high level of volatility.

This creates an extra layer of inherent risk with this strategy, and certain brokers will not let you go through with it until you have proved yourself experienced. However, this risk is mitigated to some degree as you have the possibility of earning a profit through the sale as the in the money call option will always be offset by selling the at the money options.

Once the expiration date arrives, if the price of the underlying stock drops below the strike price then all of the options are going to expire without making a profit, though they won't cost you anything extra either. If the underlying stock price ends up being greater than the in the money strike price, then you will be able to sell the option that is in the money for a profit. The amount of income that is generated by this sale will increase the closer the price is to the at the money price of the other options you purchased.

If the price of the underlying stock ends up being greater than the at the money strike price, then you will need to buy back the at the money calls to avoid losing money. As you will need to buy back more options than you are selling this will create an ever-increasing potential for loss. As such, the maximum way to generate a profit with this strategy will see the price of the underlying stock finishing up exactly at the at the money strike price. This will allow you to sell the in the money option for the greatest amount possible while still allowing the at the money calls to expire worthlessly.

CHAPTER 6: FRONT SPREAD STRATEGY

Call front spread

The front spread call strategy allows you to purchase a call that is already in the money, or slightly below the point where it would be on the money, at a discounted price. The end goal is to then gain control of the call at the initial strike price for either a small debit or even a credit through the selling of 2 calls at the second strike price. Both strike prices will need to utilize the same expiration month in order for this strategy to be effective.

When utilizing this strategy, you are going to need to be aware that it has an extremely large risk ceiling. This means you are going to need to use traditional indicators in order to determine if the time is right for this strategy in order to prevent yourself from taking a loss when the underlying asset moves more than you expect it to. This strategy is best used if you are slightly bullish about the underlying asset and you believe it will move to the second strike price and then completely stop. If the strength of the market is in question, utilizing a different strategy is recommended.

In order to achieve maximum results with this strategy, you are going to need the underlying asset price to rise from the first strike price to the second. This, in turn, provides cover for one of the calls you purchase while also leaving the second one open to the potential of even greater profits moving forward. This second call will also leave you open to additional risk if the market turns against you unexpectedly. This means you are going to want to keep a close eye on the movement of the underlying asset to ensure quick movements are countered. You will also want to include a strong stop loss situated just below the second strike point to prevent yourself from losing everything.

You can further mitigate the potential for risk through the use of index options rather than standard options. Index options are always a great choice when it comes to utilizing riskier strategies because they are the least volatile type of option you can purchase. This is due to the fact that the movement of various options in the index typically tends to cancel one another out.

To utilize this strategy, the first thing you will need to do is to purchase a call at the initial strike price. You will then want to follow this purchase up with the sale of a pair of calls that are listed at the secondary strike price. The price of the underlying stock should then ideally move enough that you make a profit from the first option while still being able to sell off the pair of calls to fund most if not all of the purchase.

When utilizing this strategy, you are going to want to keep in mind that that the closer the first call is to the expiration date, the greater your potential for profit is going to be. As such, the timeframe that is typically considered the most effective for this strategy is between 30 and 45 days. You can also utilize this strategy through the purchase of the underlying asset directly as opposed to utilizing uncovered calls which mitigate the potential risk somewhat.

Keep in mind that time decay is working in your favor through the use of this strategy. While it will still reduce the value of the option you plan on purchasing, this loss will ultimately be outweighed by the gain that will come with the pair of options you are going to sell.

Put front spread

The put front spread strategy is best used for the purchase of a put that is just at the money or slightly out of the money while not paying full price in the process. When everything works according to plan, you will be able to purchase the put at the second strike price while still earning credit or just a small debit. This extra profit comes from selling two additional puts at the first strike price.

In order for this strategy to be as effective as possible, you will need the price of the underlying asset to decrease from where it starts at the second strike price all the way to the initial strike price. This means you are going to want to utilize this strategy only when the market is feeling bearish. Additionally, you are only going to want to undertake this strategy when the indicators you favor say that the underlying asset is going to drop in price, but only a small amount. This is extremely important if you are going to come out on top as only one of your puts is covered. As such, if the stock moves dramatically you can potentially see significant losses.

This means it is very important to closely monitor the underlying asset when you utilize this strategy and never do so without having a firm stop loss in place to counter potential losses. Much like the call variation, the optimal time frame for this strategy is between 30 and 45 days from when the option will expire.

In order to utilize this strategy, you are going to want to begin by selling a pair of puts at the initial strike price. Next, you purchase a put at the secondary strike price assuming the price of the underlying asset is going to remain at or above this price.

When using this strategy, you are going to want to try and get the price of the underlying asset to end up as close to the first strike price as possible at the moment the option expires. This will ensure that you make the maximum amount of each trade. The amount of profit that you can make on the trade will be determined by the differences between the two strike prices after any net debits are taken into account. On the other hand, the maximum amount of possible loss can be determined by adding the strike prices together. If the underlying asset drops all the way down, this is what you can expect to lose.

When using this strategy, your goal should be for the implied volatility to decrease as time goes on. Doing so will decrease the value of the options you sold at twice the rate of the options you purchased, netting an overall profit.

CHAPTER 7: BACKSPREAD STRATEGY

Also known as reverse ratio spreads, backspreads are a type of option trading strategy that is best utilized when you feel that a specific underlying stock is going to experience a high degree of volatility and you have a fairly good idea of what direction the price is going to move in but aren't 100 percent convinced. If the underlying stock then moves a large amount in the direction, you predicted you would earn a large profit. If it moves in the opposite direction instead, then you will still earn a profit, though it won't be as large. However, if the underlying stock only moves a small amount, then you will see a loss instead.

Put backspread

If you are bearish on the underlying stock in question, then you are going to want to use what is known as a put backspread, or possibly a put ratio spread as put options are utilized in the strategy. To begin using this strategy, you are going to want to start by purchasing any number of put options that are currently out of the money. At the same time, you are going to want to sell a smaller number of put options that are on the money. The end result here is that you end up with a premium net credit.

While you can use any number of put options for this strategy, the simplest variation is to sell 1 in the money put option and purchase two put options that are currently out of the money. If the underlying stock then moves higher than the strike price of the in the money put option that was sold you can allow it to expire while still holding onto the credit premium as all three put options will now expire worthlessly.

If the stock price finishes up somewhere between the in the money strike price and the strike price of the pair of out of the money options, then you will lose money as you will need to buy back the in the money option and the pair of out of the money options are going to expire. However, if the price of the underlying stock drops lower than the strike price of the out of the money put option you will begin to see potentially unlimited profits as the cost of purchasing the in the money option will be greatly offset by the profits you will make selling the pair of out of the money options.

It is very important to keep in mind the fact that you cannot allow your backspread positions to expire as you will have already sold options that will need to be repurchased in order to prevent them from being exercised. As such, it is important to always ensure you have enough available funds to buy back those options in case the price of the underlying stock doesn't move.

Call backspread

Also known as the call ratio backspread, the call backspread is the type of backspread you are going to want to use if you are bullish on the underlying stock you have your eye on. The call backspread can be done by purchasing any number of out of the money call options and selling a smaller number of call options that are currently on the money. The most common way this is done is by purchasing a pair of out of the money call options and selling one call option that is currently in the money. This strategy will generate a premium as the cost of the two options will be offset by selling the third.

If the price of the underlying stock drops below the strike price, then all three of the options will expire worthlessly. You will still net the initial premium, however. If the underlying stock moves to the point that is higher than the in the money strike price but is still below the strike price of the initial calls, then you are going to lose money as the pair of calls will be worthless but you will still need to buy back the call at the in the money strike price. Once the price of the underlying stock moves past the on the money strike price, then your potential for profit really kicks into high gear. The in the money call will continue to increase in value so will need to be bought back, but this price will be mitigated by the extra gains seen from the pair of calls whose gains will keep pace with it.

CHAPTER 8: TRADING WITH
TECHNICAL INDICATORS

As the name implies, technical indicators are used in options trading as a way to determine trends as well as potential turning points in the price of underlying stocks. When used correctly, they can accurately predict movement cycles as well as determine when the most profitable time to buy or sell is going to be.

Technical indicators are typically calculated based on the price pattern of a derivative or stock. Relevant data includes closing price, opening price, lows, highs and volume. Indicators typically take the data regarding a stock's price from the past few periods depending on the charts the analyst favors and use it to generate a trend that will show what has been happening with a specific stock as well as what is likely to happen next.

Technical indicators tend to come in two main types lagging and leading. Lagging indicators are those which are based on preceding data and help to determine when a trend is forming or if a stock is currently trading in range instead. The stronger the trend the lagging indicator pinpoints, the greater the chance that it is going to continue moving forward. However, lagging indicators are of no use when it comes to determining future rally points or potential pullbacks.

Alternately, leading indicators are useful when it comes to predicting the point where the price of a given stock may rally or crash. These are typically momentum indicators which gauge the momentum of the movement the price of an underlying stock is likely to take. A momentum indicator can be thought of as the common sense that says a ball thrown into the air will not continue in the same direction forever, once it begins to slow you can accurately predict that it will soon begin to move in the opposite direction.

Leading indicators are useful when it comes to determining if the price of an underlying stock has reached an unsustainable point and when likely slowdown of a given price will occur. As stocks that are overbought or oversold are in for a pullback, having this information before the move occurs can be extremely useful when used with numerous trading strategies.

Both types of indicators are equally important as you will need to determine what types of trends are going to be forming as well be on the lookout for eventual slowdowns and pullbacks at any time in order to use many strategies successfully. Typically, you are going to want to use at least three indicators at all times.

Moving Average Convergence Divergence Indicator

The moving average convergence divergence (MACD) indicator is an oscillating indicator that typically moves between a zero point and a centerline. When used, a very high value will indicate that an underlying stock is in danger of being overbought and a consistently low value will show that the stock is oversold.

MACD charts are based on a combination of 3 different exponential moving averages (EMA). These averages can be based on any period, though the most common are the 12-26-9 chart. The first part of this chart is generally listed as the 12-day and 26-day EMA. The 12-day EMA is the faster of the two.

Using a faster and a slower EMA allows you to accurately gauge the momentum of the trend you are following. If the 12-day EMA is above the 26-day EMA, then you can assume the underlying stock is in an uptrend while the reverse is also true. When the 12-day EMA increases at a rate that is much greater than that of the 26-day EMA, then the uptrend is likely to become more pronounced. When the 12-day EMA begins to slow and draws close to the 26-day EMA, then the trend's momentum is going to fade letting you know the uptrend will end soon.

The MACD makes use of these 2 EMAs by looking at the difference between them and plotting that difference. If the 12-day and the 26-day are the same, then the MACD will be 0. If the 12-day is higher than the 26-day, then the MACD will be positive and vice versa. The greater the difference between the pair, the further the MACD line will be from the centerline (if positive) or zero (if negative).

On its own, this line doesn't provide that much more information than a standard moving average. It becomes much more useful when the 9-day EMA is added to the mix. The 9-day EMA is different than the others in that it is the EMA of the MACD line, not of a stock price. This EMA then acts as the other EMA lines and smooths out the MACD line to make its results more manageable.

There is also a more complicated way to use the MACD indicator which is known as the MACD histogram. The histogram can be thought of like the difference between the MACD line and the 9-day EMA. When the MACD line crosses above the 9-day EMA, the MACD histogram will cross above 0 which indicates a bullish signal. If it crosses below 0, then it indicates a bearish trend. When charted, if the histogram forms a series of descending peaks this is known as a negative divergence with a positive divergence being indicated by a series of ascending peaks.

When a negative divergence occurs, it is a sign that the current positive uptrend is likely to reverse sooner than later. This can happen even if the pattern of the underlying stock price itself seems to be moving higher and higher on the chart. The reverse is also true. These signals can become somewhat muddy when the price trades at the range for a prolonged period of time which is why it is important to always use multiple indicators to avoid seeing false signals.

Average directional index

The average directional index acts as a type of guide that confirms the signals generated by other technical indicators you may choose to use. Once a trend is identified, the average directional index can determine its relative strength. The average directional index is a combination of both the positive and negative directional indicators which track upward and downward trends respectively. The average directional index then combines them into a unified way to determine the relative strength of a trend.

The average directional index is an oscillating indicator with a range between 0 and 100. Zero indicates a flat trend with virtual no volatility while 100 indicates that a given stock is moving practically straight up or down with a large degree of volatility. This indicator only measures the relative strength of the trend, it will not tell you which direction it is likely to move in.

In general, you will want to keep in mind that average directional index values rarely reach above 60 as trends of this strength typically only appear in long recession or very long runs when the market is bullish. As such, a value that is greater than 40 can be considered a vibrant trend while a value below 20 means that the underlying stock is in what is known as a trading range.

When it comes to signals that are produced by the average directional index, if a trend moves from above 40 to below then you can deduce that the trend is slowing which is a bad sign for most popular options trading strategies. As such, if you see this movement occur you can assume that it is time to close out your existing positions. On the other hand, if you see a trend move from below 20 to a point somewhere above it then you can assume that the sideways market movement is coming to an end and a new major trend is going to soon be forming. Depending on the direction of the trend you will then be able to decide if you need to adopt a strategy that is bearish or one that is bullish.

Additionally, you can also determine useful information when it comes to the point where the positive directional index and the negative directional index cross paths. When the positive directional index crosses above the negative directional index from below then you can assume the signal is bullish. When the negative directional index crosses above the positive directional index from below then you know that the trend is going to be bearish instead.

Regardless of the strength of the trends, you find it is recommended that you never base your options trade on just one indicator. Ideally, you will want to use at least three in order to confirm the signals you are seeing aren't flukes and to ensure you prevent false alarms.

CHAPTER 9: WEEKLY OPTIONS TRADING

Weekly options are those that are listed for the purpose of providing short-term trading along with ample opportunities for hedging. As the name implies, they expire every week. They are listed on Thursday and expire the next Friday. Weekly options have been around for years but were traditionally only traded by investors working in cash indices. This all changed in 2011 when the number of ways that weekly options could be traded was expanded by the Chicago Board of Options. While at first there were only 28 underlying stocks that qualified to be traded weekly, that number has now grown to over 800.

In addition to their timeframe, weekly options differ from traditional options in other ways as well. There is one week of every month when weekly options are not available. They are also not listed as part of the monthly options expiration style. Technically the week that monthly options expire they are the same as weekly options.

Weekly option advantages

Trading weekly options come with several advantages. First and foremost, purchasing weekly options provides you with the opportunity to buy exactly what you need with less upfront capital required. As such, if you are looking for a swing trade for just a few days or even a day trade, weekly options are the right choice. For sellers, weekly options all you to sell more frequently as opposed to just once per month.

Weekly options trades also allow you to reduce the cost of trades that have a long-term spread including diagonal spreads and calendar spreads because you can then sell weekly options against them. High volume traders can also use weekly options as a way to hedge larger portfolios and positions against the risk that comes along with certain events. When the market at large is range bound, the weekly options market can still be utilized for strategies including the iron condor and butterflies of multiple types.

Weekly option disadvantages

The quick expiration date of weekly options means that you won't have much time for the market to turn around if you make a poor choice. If you are selling options, it is important to be aware that the gamma for them is going to be much more sensitive than with traditional options. As such, if you are shorting options then a small overall move can turn an option that is just out of the money into one which is deep in the money extremely quickly.

Weekly options require much more active risk management. If you do not take the time to properly size your trades and lock your profits, they can drain your trade balance quickly. Additionally, implied volatility is going to be much higher because of the timeframe as well. Near-term options are always going to be more vulnerable when it comes to dramatic price swings.

Buying weekly calls/puts

As you have a much more limited amount of time to turn a profit, your timing when purchasing a weekly call or put needs to be spot on. If you choose poorly when it comes to price direction, strike selection and timeframe you can easily end up sitting on an option that is completely worthless. You will need to be aware of your level of risk aversion because while the cost is going to be cheaper, you will generally want to purchase a greater number of options each week.

Ideally, you are going to want to avoid naked call or put options with weekly calls as they tend to be low probability trades. If you have a bias towards a specific direction, then a structured trade or a debit spread is often preferable.

Selling weekly calls and puts

Selling weekly options can generate a reliable amount of success in the long term. You are defining your profit margins up front, however, so it is important to have a firm idea of what your options are worth to avoid selling yourself short. Selling weekly trades will allow you to collect the full premium if you guess correctly but exposes you to undefined losses if you choose poorly which requires an extra margin.

The best types of underlying stocks for these trades are lower priced as they each take up a smaller amount of your overall buying power. It is also easier to bet on high implied volatility as it is more likely to revert to the mean in the given timeframe. As a rule, selling a put in the short term is preferable to selling a call as it tends to generate a higher return in the weekly market.

Spreads

Selling an option and purchasing an option that is further in the money is a great way to take advantage of the weekly market. As the overall implied level of volatility is much higher in the weekly market, the spread can help you in case the direction reverses unexpectedly before you have a chance to do anything about it. Selling an option against the long option naturally, reduces the role implied volatility would have on the successful trade. Ideally, you will want to use a debit spread near the point where the current price is sitting and aim for a 1 to 1 trade when it comes to risk and reward.

Butterfly spread

This is an ideal trade to make when the implied volatility is at its maximum. The body of the butterfly benefits from the decrease in implied volatility moving forward while the underlying stays near the short strikes. Buying them is typically going to be more effective as well because you can typically pick them up at the weekly market for what amounts to 0 additional cost or possibly a small debit. This strategy is particularly effective if used just prior to an earnings announcement as you can still earn money from the credit even if you bet on the wrong direction or the trend doesn't extend as far as you expected.

CONCLUSION

Thank you for making it through to the end of *Options Trading: Strategies on How to Excel at Options Trading*, let's hope it was informative and able to provide you with all of the tools you need to achieve your options trading goals, whatever it is that they may be. Just because you've finished this book doesn't mean there is nothing left to learn on the topic, expanding your horizons is the only way to find the mastery you seek.

New option trading strategies and technical indicators are always being developed, and it is important that you continue to seek them out as you never know when you might stumble across a new favorite. Above all else it is important to avoid resting on your laurels as being satisfied with your overall skill level is really just the first step to letting the competition get a leg up on you.

The next step is to stop reading already and to get ready to try out all the strategies you have learned. While many traders may recommend practicing with a dummy account first, a better solution is to practice with low-value trades instead. Practicing with a dummy account doesn't allow you to practice your trading mindset which means that when you get back out into the real world, you will have to deal with potential pitfalls that can turn a strategy that worked quite well with the pretend trades into something of a nightmare when used in the real world.

Take it slow and always take small, reliable returns over the potential of huge, risky windfalls. Never risk more in a given trade than you can afford to lose and before you know it you will be a successful veteran options trader. Remember, successful options trading is a marathon, not a sprint, slow and steady wins the race.

I would be so grateful if you please leave me a review ☺. I would love to get your feedback.

Sign up to my mailing list below to be the first to be notified of the release of my next book coming out shortly! ☺

Also when you sign-up please feel free to send me an e-mail with your opinion and suggestions. I would love to hear from you!

Sign Up & Join
<u>Andrew Johnson's</u>
<u>Mailing List!</u>

*EXCLUSIVE UPDATES

*FREE BOOKS

*NEW REALEASE ANNOUCEMENTS BEFORE ANYONE ELSE GETS THEM

*DISCOUNTS

*GIVEAWAYS

FOR NOTIFACTIONS OF MY <u>*NEW RELEASES*</u> :

Never miss my next FREE PROMO, my next NEW RELEASE or a GIVEAWAY!

Made in the USA
San Bernardino, CA
11 December 2017